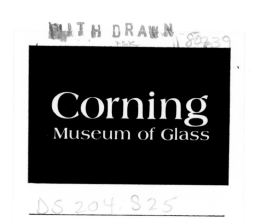

His Majesty the late King
Abdulaziz bin Abdulrahman Al Saud,
Founder of The Kingdom of Saudi Arabia

His Majesty the Late King Faisal bin Abdulaziz

His Majesty King Khalid bin Abdulaziz

His Royal Highness Crown Prince Fahad bin Abdulaziz
Deputy Prime Minister

An introduction to:

Saudi Arabian Antiquities

Department of Antiquities and Museums
Ministry of Education - Kingdom of Saudi Arabia
1395 A.H - 1975 A.D

photography by
Roger Wood

Issued by:

Department of Antiquities and Museums
Ministry of Education - Kingdom of Saudi Arabia
1395 A.H - 1975 A.D

Table of contents

Foreword

It is reasonable to assume that human beings normally feel attached to their homeland, possess the desire to serve it and wish to see it stand alongside the other distinguished nations of the world. In order for these sentiments to flourish healthily, however, they must be tended with care and guided through the enlightenment of education so that their roots may deepen.

A person's knowledge of his homeland, particularly those unique qualities and characteristics that set it apart from other nations, must be balanced by knowledge of his country's past, for to be comprehended the present must be viewed through the perspective of historical reality. The various types of recorded literary achievements and oral traditions are not the only intellectual heritage of a people: material antiquities also accrue to their present intellectual wealth. And as evidences of the past, the relics of antiquity, especially when found in their original context, afford a more tangible view of historical reality that can be readily comprehended by the onlooker. Moreover, successive generations of researchers can apply to them a variety of analytical methods from which to glean answers to many different theoretical questions. Clearly, material antiquities, when properly recovered and assessed, are the most valuable means of shedding light on the detailed dimensions, obscurities and mysteries of the past.

How do the antiquities of a country serve to enhance a sentiment of national pride and commitment? In beholding the tangible, positive achievements of his forebears, a person can come to appreciate the greatness of his country's past, and upon reflecting on the vastly extended resources available to him today, can ascertain the progress that his nation has achieved in its continuing development. Undoubtedly, such understanding greatly contributes to the growth of commitment and dedication towards exellence in the members of the contemporary generation.

The Arabian Peninsula has always been a birthplace of many civilizations. Countless monuments are still standing today that attest to the existence of various centers once widespread in the Peninsula. In the Kingdom of Saudi Arabia there are remains of several such civilizational centers and at the present time efforts are being made to document and survey them in preparation for their proper excavation and recovery. In addition, several museums are being planned and built to accomodate the growing corpus of data.

In this book, which it pleases me to introduce to those interested in some aspects of Saudi Arabia's history, the Department of Antiquities and Museums in the Ministry of Education presents a synoptic view of the various antiquities in the country. The illustrations include only the exposed and/or haphazardly found antiquities. Much still remains to be known through future controlled recovery. As such, the book is truly a prolegomenon for the countless researches and efforts that will follow in the near future. I wish those involved in these endeavors every success.

Dr. Abdulaziz al-Khowaiter
Minister of Education
President, High Council for Antiquities

Acknowledgments

The realization of this book, in both its Arabic and English versions, is the result of the collaboration of many individuals, both inside and outside the Department of Antiquities.

It is with pleasure that the authorities of the Ministry of Education and the Department of Antiquities acknowledge the services of Department personnel in the compilation of the book, many of these performed above and beyond the call of duty. Particular recognition is due to Mr. Ahmed H. Sharaf ad-Din, the Department epigrapher, who obligingly prepared reference texts and translated some hitherto unpublished inscriptions. Dr. Juris Zarins, archaeological advisor of the Department, undertook extensive research to supply background information for the preparation of textual material. The detailed geographical maps are the result of the efforts of Mr. Salah al-Helwah, the Department's surveyor. Preliminary drafts in Arabic were typed by Mr. Mokhtar Ahmed Mustafa.

Outside the department, Dr. Abdulrahman al-Ansari, Professor of Archaeology and chairman of the Department of History at Riyadh University, kindly read through the textual material and made very valuable suggestions, many of which were incorporated into the final draft. He also generously supplied background information and photographs of his ongoing fruitful research at the important site of al-Fau.

We wish especially to express our appreciation to the photographer, Mr. Roger Wood, whose valuable cooperation in the course of the performance of his duties was also significant in the process of the selection of illustrations. Credit for the composition of the English captions and the editing of the English Text goes to C.M. Piesinger.

Finally, we would like to thank the printing company, Amilcare Pizzi, and especially the Managing Director, Mr. Fulvio Nembrini, for the cooperative spirit in which they have weathered with us the difficulties of bringing about the project.

On behalf of HE Dr. Abdulaziz al-Khowaiter, Minister of Education, and HRH Prince Khalid bin Fahad bin Khalid, deputy Minister of Education, we wish to offer our thanks to all of the above as well as to many others for whom space does not allow mention here.

Any errors of fact or interpretation which may occur will, of course, be our own responsibility.

Introduction

The kingdom of Saudi Arabia embraces the major portion of the Arabian Peninsula. It is a land whose antiquities and early heritage have yet even to be outlined, let alone critically analyzed.

The great antiquity of human settlement in the Peninsula has actually never been suspect; indeed, historical conjectures have always pictured Arabia as the original homeland of the diverse groups of people who populated the ancient Near East in early historical times. Now, recently compiled data, coupled with chance discoveries, have augmented this view of ancient Arabia. Future research promises to confirm the impression that the Peninsula was a source of significant contributions to the rise of the earliest civilization of mankind, that of southern Mesopotamia. When one considers that from within its confines came the call to Islam, a religion and world view which has shaped the history of the entire Near East and influenced the destinies of lands and peoples even further afield, it is easy to conjecture for Arabia the existence of a human heritage of comparable significance during its more remote antiquity. It seems certain that with the unraveling of the mysteries of her ancient past which will be effected by future scientific investigation, Greater Arabia stands to contribute much to our knowledge of human history and of pristine civilizational processes.

In realization of the importance of such research, the government of the Kingdom of Saudi Arabia, under the eminent leadership of His Majesty the late King Faisal (may he rest in peace) has founded and generously supported a Department of Antiquities. It was initiated in the early 1960's and is a branch of the Ministry of Education. More recently, the earnest necessity for protection and preservation of the Kingdom's antiquities led to the drawing up of a comprehensive set of Antiquities Regulations, which were issued as part of a Royal Decree. The Decree also provided for the formation of a High Council for Antiquities, presided over by the Minister of Education and his Deputy, and composed of highly-placed persons from other concerned government agencies and local scholars of history and antiquities. The Council has been charged with the setting of the broad policies governing research and preservation of antiquities.

The Council has already adopted a series of important rulings and programs related to the study and preservation of the archeological heritage of the kingdom. The major programs currently underway include the following:

A. THE SURVEY PROGRAM

A comprehensive archaeological survey of the kingdom is to be launched over the span of the next five years. Its aim will be to document all archaelogical sites, monuments, and other remains which date from the beginnings of human settlement in Arabia to the recent past. The decision of the Council to effect this survey is a result of its strongly-held belief that such systematic accumulation of archaeological data through a controlled program is a necessary prerequisite to any serious detailed investigation of the antiquities of the kingdom.

B. DARB ZUBAIDAH PROJECT

Saudi Arabia's unique position as the heartland of the Islamic heritage is to be given due attention by a decision to preserve, restore and eventually partially reutilize the most significant Islamic architectural monument of the kingdom, the *Darb Zubaida*, or Pilgrims' Road, which dates to the early Golden Age of Islam.

C. THE DARIYYAH PROJECT

The historic process which led to the foundation of the modern kingdom is to be illuminated by the restoration and revitalization of Dariyyah, the town wherein was centered the religio-political pact between the reformer, Imam Mohammad Ibn Abdul-Wahab and the House of Ibn Saud.

D. ESTABLISHMENT OF MUSEUMS

The Council has strongly recommended a plan to found a National Central Museum in the capital city of Riyadh, for the eventual purpose of the exhibition of the potentially vast material components of the cultural heritage of the kingdom. This will replace the temporary museum established in 1966. In addition, a plan has been approved to found half a dozen regional museums in the major cities of the country, and several local museums at principal archaeological sites. With regard to their unique status, a specialized Islamic museum will be established in each of the holy cities of Islam: Mecca and Medina.

E. DISSEMINATION OF ARCHAEOLOGICAL INFORMATION

In realization of the ultimate need for a medium of scientific communication on the progress of research in the field of archaeology within the kingdom, the Council has approved the publication of a scientific journal devoted to historical and archaeological studies. This formal publication will be established concurrently with the advent of the survey program. In the meantime, the Council has urged the issue of generalized publications on the antiquities of the Kingdom, of which the present volume is an example.

The aim of this book is to present a broad (primarily illustrated) introduction to the archaeological sites and monuments within the confines of the Kingdom. As such, it bears no claim to any definitive statements on the nature and/or extent of the cultural components involved. At best it is meant to serve as a guide to some of the archaeological remains which represent an undoubtedly complex and involved history of occupation in Greater Arabia.

Since, however, some parts of the Kingdom are relatively better-known archaeologically than others, either because of detailed study or by analogy to similar components in adjacent countries, certain information in this volume is to be accepted as validly tested. In order to serve as a guide to the record of scientific archaeological research which has been done in the kingdom up to the present, a summary of such is presented below.

A. Principal contemporary Saudi scholars concerned specifically with the study of Arabian antiquities:
1. *Shaikh Abdul-Quddus Al-Ansari*
   He has conducted valuable research on the history of occupation in and around the holy lands of Mecca and Medina, and is also widely published in this field.
2. *Shaikh Hamad Al-Jasir*
   This eminant Nejdi scholar of history and archaeology has published a treatise on an archaeological journey in northwest Arabia which is one of the principal sources of information on that area.
3. *Shaikh Abdullah Ibn Khamis*
   A well-published scholar of history and archaeology, he has undertaken and published an

account of an archaeological journey between the regions of Nejd in central Arabia and the Hejaz in the west and northwest.

4. *Dr. Abdulrahman al-Ansari*

Dr. Ansari, the former dean of the faculty of Arts at the University of Riyadh, is one of the leading pioneers of scientific archaeology in the kingdom. His epigraphic work on early north-western scripts is of considerable importance. More significantly, in the fall of 1972 he inaugurated the first University-sponsored archaeological field project at the site of Al-Fau, a well-known ancient central Arabian emporium. This ongoing investigation has already resulted in the recovery of very valuable information concerning social and economic life in the heart of Arabia around the second half of the first millennium B.C. Dr. Ansari's efforts have also helped to create a forum for archaeological research by the establishment of a quasi-academic Society for History and Archaeology within the Faculty of Arts at Riyadh University. The society has sponsored the opening of the first University-based Museum of Archaeology.

5. *Dr. Abdullah H. Masry*

Dr. Masry, the author of this introduction, is the present Director of Antiquities and Museums in the kingdom. He has investigated the prehistoric Ubaid component of the eastern region of the country, with special emphasis on the significance of the area at this time to developments in southern Iraq which were to lead to the beginnings of civilization. The results of this work have recently been published.

B. Foreign scholars and institutions who have undertaken archaeological or epigraphic research within the kingdom with the cooperation of the Department of Antiquities:

1. *Expedition of the Universities of Toronto and Kentucky*

Under the joint direction of Drs. Fred Winnett and William Reed, this expedition undertook a survey of a total area of 1800 square miles in the northern part of the kingdom in 1962. The results were published under the title *Ancient Records from North Arabia*. One of the important discoveries made by the expedition was a rock inscription found on the top of Jebel Ghunaim near the ancient Arabian city of Taima. The inscription contains a reference to the deity *Salm* mentioned in the famous Taima stone (now at the Louvre). This stone documents the surrender of the last Neo-Babylonian king, Nabonidus, to the Achaemenid forces.

Dr. Winnett also returned to north central Arabia in 1967 and undertook a survey of the Hail region. Results of this work were published under the title *An Archaeological-Epigraphical Survey of the Hail Area of Northern Saudi Arabia*.

2. *Epigraphical work of Professors Ruth Stiehl and Albert Jamme - 1966 and 1968*

These works dealt primarily with inscriptions and rock carvings in the regions of the Hejaz in the west and Midian in the northwest. The areas around Madain Saleh, Ula, Hannakia and Taif were also covered, although less extensively. The work was largely a follow-up of an earlier comprehensive survey undertaken by the two French explorers, Jaussen and Savignac, in the early part of this century.

3. *Survey of the Danish Expedition in Eastern Arabia - 1968*

This brief foray into eastern Arabia was but one part of the long and extensive involvement of the Danish Expedition in the Arabian Gulf. It was conducted primarily to investigate the location of the renowned Seleucid emporium of Gerrha. The preliminary results of the survey have been published under the title *Preliminary Survey in East Arabia*.

4. *Survey of the University of London in Northwestern Arabia - 1968*

The area covered in this survey, led by Professor Peter Parr of the Institute of Archaeology, extended along the northwestern coast of the Red Sea to just north of Medina, and penetrated into the interior to a depth of 300 km. A number of Late Bronze Age, Nabatean, Roman and Islamic sites were recorded and briefly studied. The results were published under the title *Preliminary Survey in NW Arabia.*

5. *The Smithsonian Institutions Expedition - 1968*

Directed by Mr. Gus Van Beek, this very brief project entailed a survey of the southwestern reaches of the country, with special emphasis on the Nejran-Ukhdud area. Various sites, spanning the time from the late Stone Age to the Islamic period, were recorded. Although the results have not been published, a report exists which is entitled *Preliminary Archaeological Survey of Wadi Nejran.*

The plan followed in the presentation of the contents of this book reflects the regional geographic divisions of the Kingdom, working from the southwest to the north and east in a clockwise direction. Each geographic zone, which is nearly identical with a historic regional division, is taken as a unit. What is known to date of its history of human settlement is then chronologically presented, along with a description of any artifacts which have so far been recovered from it.

Such treatment proceeds under the assumption that the various geographic regions of Greater Arabia have had fundamentally different experiences with regard to settlement and contact. The historic central cultural core of Greater Arabia has always possessed great homogeneity. The peripheries, on the other hand, were involved in significant cultural dialogues with lands beyond the peninsula. As a consequence, at any given time their cultural profiles were a function of the degree of such contact. The prediction that the emergence of a clearer picture of the antiquity of peripheral Arabia (supported by its core) will necessitate a rewriting of the processual outline of the rise of pristine civilization in the Near East is no idle speculation. Present archaeological evidence, though still sketchy, gives great promise of the confirmation of this prediction.

The eastern and northeastern flanks of Greater Arabia, for instance, may well have made significant contributions to the shaping of the earliest culture of Mesopotamia, the birthplace of civilization. Later, the region appears to have acted as an intermediary in complex economic and social relationships between the centers of civilization situated to its north and east. Northern Arabia, meanwhile, may have carried out important contacts and relationships with the Syrio-Palestinian and Mediterranean littoral complex, while the west and northwest were clearly in a good position to form dialogues with and influence events in Egypt. In the southwest, where we have evidence of the rise of high centers of urban civilization as early as the second millennium B.C., the cultural profile was of a decisively different order from that of any other region. The southwest may also prove to be a region of tremendous significance as regards Early Man, due to its proximity to and virtual identity with the geologic-geographic configuration of East Africa. In the heart of Arabia, however, amid the vast seas of chaotic sand, one may look forward to the unveiling of an antiquity which reflects the pristine components of a truly indigenous Arabian cultural complex.

Director of Antiquities
and Museums
Dr. Abdullah H. Masry

رسم متقن لجواد ، نحت على حجر من جدار
أحد المباني الرئيسية في موقع الأخدود
بنجران الذي يعود تاريخه الى القرن الثاني
ق . م . ٠

Figure of a horse carved on a stone of one of the main buildings at Ukhdud, outside Nejran. This pre-Islamic/early Islamic site dates from around the 2nd century B.C.-5th century A.D.

The southwestern region
Asir and Nejran

The southwestern region of the kingdom is composed of the highland of Asir and the narrow coastal strip of Tehama. The early history of this region is closely linked with that of Yemen and the rest of South Arabia, or *Arabia Felix* proper.

Although very little is yet known about the extent and depth of early occupation in the area, several monumental sites are known which establish a distinguished antiquity for the region. These include settlements in the Wadi Nejran, the site of Nejran itself (and the nearby famous site of Ukhdud), and Jarash, near the modern settlement of Khamis Mushait. Elsewhere, along the Wadi Bisha south of Taif, and along the historic route which leads from the southwest toward the north and east and skirts the Wadi Dawasir and the Tuwaiq escarpment, there can be found thousands of early inscriptions, rock drawings and graffiti.

NEJRAN

Nejran was an important early town situated along the trade route which historically connected South Arabia with the north. It is located in the large wadi bearing the same name, some 300 km. south of Abha, the regional capital of Asir. The town was mentioned in a Sabaean text dating to the 7th century B.C. in the context of its having been conquered and annexed by the then ruling Sabaean king, Karb al-Watar. Strabo described Nejran as the Town of the Seven Walls during the aborted Roman campaign against southern Arabia in the 1st century A.D.

Aside from the main settlement at Ukhdud, several pre-Islamic sites are known along the Wadi Nejran, such as the Qarya Qadimah, the Jebel Ajamah ruins, and Ukhdud South. At Ukhdud itself impressive ashlar masonry structures, as well as the remnants of a large surrounding wall, still stand to an appreciable height.

JARASH

Jarash is located 240 km. to the north of Nejran, and is distinguished by the ruins of a substantial pre-Islamic settlement, several South Arabic inscriptions, and, on the small outcrop of Jebel Hamumah behind the settlement, a number of rock drawings of human and animal figures. Istakhri speaks of both Nejran and Jarash as having been important centers for the production of leather goods.

منظر عام لأطلال الاخدود ، ويظهر مبنى المعبد فى وسط الصورة .

Ukhdud: general view of the inner area of the site, with the ruins of the temple visible in the middle ground.

كتل حجرية ضخمة جيدة الصقل تكون احدى حجرات معبد الأخدود .

Closeup of the interior of the temple shown above. Note the extremely large slabs on which can be seen excellent examples of the marginal drafting technique.

منظريوضح الدقة فى صقل الكتل الحجرية التى استعملت فى مبانى الأخدود .

Detail of masonry at Ukhdud, exhibiting a marginal drafting technique on the large slab, a style of stone-cutting unique to South Arabia.

رسم منحوت لثعبانين ملتويين (اعلا) ،
و نقش بالخط السبئى ، كلاهما على جدار
خارجية فى الاخدود .

A carved figure depicting inter-
twined snakes and a Sabaean inscription decorate stone blocks of
the temple at Ukhdud.

منظر تفصيلى لبقايا حوائط خارجية فى
الأخدود .

Ukhdud: detail of masonry.

جدار خارجى فى الاخدود نحتت عليه نقوش
سبئية ورسم لجمل (على الصفحة السابقة)

overleaf
Outer wall of Ukhdud temple: Sabaean inscriptions and the figure
of a camel.

منظر تفصيلي لداخل احدى حجرات مباني
الاخدود .

Closeup of the architecture of the
interior of a room in the inner area
of the site at Ukhdud.

الأخدود :
تفصيل لرسم يد انسان نحتت على الصخر .
منظر عام للموقع ، و يظهر جزء من وادي
نجران في اعلا الصورة .

Ukhdud: impression of a human
hand carved on a stone block.
General view of the site showing
Wadi Nejran and the modern town
in the background.

منجر ضخم من الحجر .
رحى حجرية .

Milling stones and a huge mortar-
like instrument carved out of solid
stone.

جرش :
اطلال المباني الاسلامية .

Jarash: outline of buildings of the Islamic period, with the modern village in the background.

منجر من الحجر بجانب اطلال المباني .

Carved stone "mortar", placed up-side-down.

منظر عام لموقع مدينة جرش .

General view of the site of Jarash, famed in pre-Islamic and early Islamic times for the manufacture of leather goods. Jebel Hamumah, seen in the background, bears several inscriptions and graffiti contemporary with the occupation of the site.

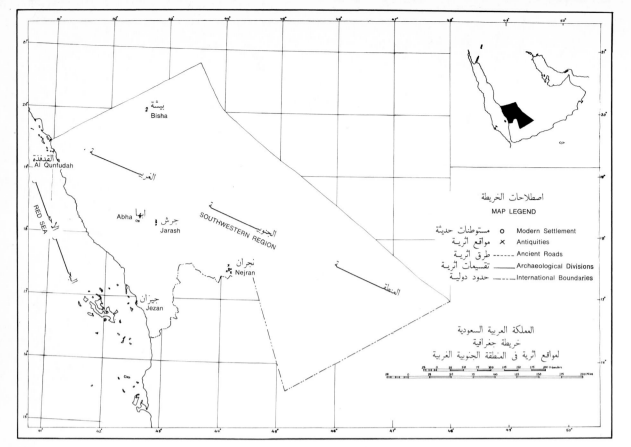

Geographical Map of the Archaeological Sites in the Southwestern Region.

اصطلاحات الخريطة
MAP LEGEND

○   Modern Settlement   مستوطنات حديثة
×   Antiquities   مواقع أثرية
----   Ancient Roads   طرق أثرية
——   Archaeological Divisions   تقسيمات أثرية
-·-·-   International Boundaries   حدود دولية

المملكة العربية السعودية
خريطة جغرافية
لمواقع أثرية فى المنطقة الجنوبية الغربية

المنطقـة الجنوبيـة الغربيـة

عسير ــ نجران

يرتبط تاريخ وآثار هذه المنطقة ارتباطا وثيقا بحضارة مأسماه الاغريق والرومان «ببلاد العرب السعيدة» (اليمن القديم) التى تعتبر بحق أحد المعاقل الرئيسيه لحضارة الشرق القديم . وكانت تمر بالمنطقة أهم الطرق التجارية التى كانت تربط جنوب الجزيرة بشمالها ، وشمالها الشرقى كطريق نجران ــ الطائف ــ مكه ، وطريق نجران ــ الفاو ــ الخليج العربى ، وكلاهما كانتا تمران بجبال عسير . ويعود تاريخ الطريق التجارى عبر عسير الى بداية القرن الأول للميلاد ، وهو التاريخ الذى بدأت فيه تهجر الطريق الشرقية التى كانت تمر عبر الصحراء وحل محلها الطريق الجبلى .

نجــران

أهم المدن الحضارية القديمة فى المنطقة حيث كانت تربط بين شمال الجزيرة العربيه بجنوبها منذ أقدم الأزمنة . وتقع المدينة فى وادى نجران الفسيح الذى يجرى بين جبال عاليـه وينطلق من الجنوب الغربى الى الشمال الشرقى ثم يتجه شرقا حيث ينحسر فى صحراء رملةيام . وأهـم الاطلال الأثريه فى نجران الحديثه هى الأخدود ، القرية القديمه ، مواقع جبل عجامة ، وموقع الأخدود الجنوبى ، ولاتزال بقايا سور الاخدود وقصوره موجودة على شكل مبانى وأنقاض تحمل رسوما فنية رائعة ونقوشا معينية وسبئية وكوفية . وقد جاء ذكر نجران فى نقش الملك السبئى كرب ال وثار (القرن السابع قبل الميلاد) كواحدة من المدن التى غزاها . وسماها سترابون (المؤرخ الرومانى) بالآبار السبع عند ما وصف معركة جرت بين الرومان و بين أهلها ابان حملة ايلوس غالوس (القرن الأول للميلاد). وقد غزاها ذو نواس الملك الحميرى (القرن الخامس للميلاد) فى حادثة الاخدود المذكورة فى القرآن الكريم . وقبل ظهور الاسلام كانت نجران مجرد أبرشية للنصارى من أشهر اساقفتهم قس بن ساعدة الأيادى ، الخطيب العربى المشهور .

جــرش

مدينة أثرية قديمة تعود الى عصر ماقبل الاسلام وبعده واشتهرت بدبغ الجلود وتصديرها . تقع خارج مدينة خميس مشيط وتبعد عـن أبهـا مسافة ٧٥ كيلو متـرا شمالا . وكانت على الطريق التجارى الذى اخترق جبال السراة من نجران الى الطائف شمالا . أما اليوم فلم يبق منها سوى اطلال سورها ومبانيها المطمورة تحت سطح الأرض . ومن أثارها الأحجار الكبيرة المنحوته ، والنقوش والرسومات المختلفه على صخور جبل حمومة الواقع خلفها .

منظر عام لأعلى وادى الثعلى جنوب الطائف حيث يقعسد السملقى المشهور والذى يعتقد أن يعود تاريخ بنائه الى فترة ماقبل الاسلام .

Sed Samallagi, a pre-Islamic/early Islamic dam 35 km. south of Taif, once controlled water in the Wadi Liyyah. Here, a general view of the valley containing the dam.

The western region
The Hejaz

The western region of Saudi Arabia, (also known as the Hejaz) contains most of the historic monuments which are of special significance to Arab/Islamic traditions. In addition to the primary mosques at Mecca and Medina, numerous monuments and historic landmarks in the Hejaz record the struggles of the prophet Mohammed and his faithful companions during the period surrounding the birth of Islam. With regard to their special nature, a separate publication devoted to the monuments of the Holy Lands will be issued subsequently.

Listed below are examples of some of the pre-Islamic to early Islamic archaeological monuments of the western region (outside the Holy Lands) with special emphasis on the area around Taif, 70 km. west of Mecca.

SED SAMALLAGI

This is a substantial dam constructed of unmortared stones and located in Wadi Liyyah, c. 30 km. south of Taif. The dam is thought to have been built in pre-Islamic times, but to have continued in use until the Islamic Middle Ages, when it is known to have collapsed.

The dam was built to store water from rains which would cause flash-floods in the wadi. It is 10 m. wide, with a plastered top, and measures over 200 m. in length. As the dam retained water on the upstream side, it could be slowly released for the irrigation of farms downstream. At present, however, the wadi has broken through the dam and slips through a gorge. On top of the rocky outcrops overlooking Sed Samallagi stand two **mintars**, or watchtowers, which are probably contemporaneous with the dam.

UKAZ SUK

Ukaz, located 40 km. north of Taif, was the site of the largest and most well-known of the pre-Islamic **suks**, or gathering places. These **suks** were the scenes of annual gatherings held for commercial, political and social purposes, as well as for the competitive recitation of poetry and prose.

The series of building remains visible on the site includes prominent outlines of walls of basaltic stone, which in some cases are surmounted by courses of mud-brick. The **suk** continued to be in use during early Islamic times, and some of the structures date to the Abbasid Period (c. 8th century A.D.). Way-stations on the Pilgrims' Road, located nearby, are probably associated with these structures. In the year 129 A.H. (760 A.D.) a hostile sectarian group invaded and pillaged the site.

BIRKAT AL-KHURABAH

Birkat al-Khurabah is one of the pools built along the **Darb Zubaida**, or Pilgrim's Road, and is located 95 km. north of Taif. This road and its accommodations were established at the initiative of Lady Zubaida, wife of the Abbasid caliph, Harun al-Rashid (c. 740 A.D.). It connected the Holy Lands of Arabia with southern Iraq by means of a string of about 50 way-stations. In addition to the pools, these stations contained extensive buildings, including palaces ond other structures, for the temporary housing of high functionaries, ordinary pilgrims and caravan crews.

The pool at Khurabah, built of basalt, is circular in shape and has a maximum depth of 6 meters. Twenty-one steps lead down into it. A small structure sits astride the pool, and a settling basin, also built of basalt, is situated alongside. Water enters the pool through a long sluice leading from Wadi Aqiq, some 25 km. away. The pool has recently been partially reconstructed for the use of the surrounding modern villages.

Upstream view of the dam looking
north, with contemporary *mintar*
(watchtower) in left background.
Note construction technique of
building in successive horizontal
sections.

تفصيل للكتل الحجرية الضخمة التى استخدمت
فى بناء السد ، ويبلغ طول بعضها حوالى المتر .

Sed Samallagi — detail of construction technique: dry-stone wall-
ing using large unshaped boulders
chinked with small stones.

منظر شامل لسطح سد السملقى الذى
يبلغ عرضه حوالى ١٠ أمتار و يمتد لمسافة
٢٠٠ متر طولا .

Panoramic view of the top of Sed
Samallagi, looking southeast. The
dam is 10 meters wide and over
200 meters long.

منظر بانورامى لأسفل السد ، ويلاحظ
التدرج فى نظام البناء .

Downstream view of Sed Samallagi. Note stepped pattern of the
stonework.

منظر عام لموقع عكاظ قرب الحوية .

General view of the most probable location of Ukaz Suq, a pre-Islamic/Islamic forum for literature and other functions.

اطلال بعض المباني في عكاظ والتي ينسب بناؤها الى العصر العباسي

Ukaz Suq: roughly faced stone wall of main structure on the site (Abbasid date - c. 7th-8th centuries A.D.).

بقايا أحد الأسوار الحجرية في عكاظ .

Remains of a large wall at Ukaz Suq, constructed of the native basalt with cement-like mortar.

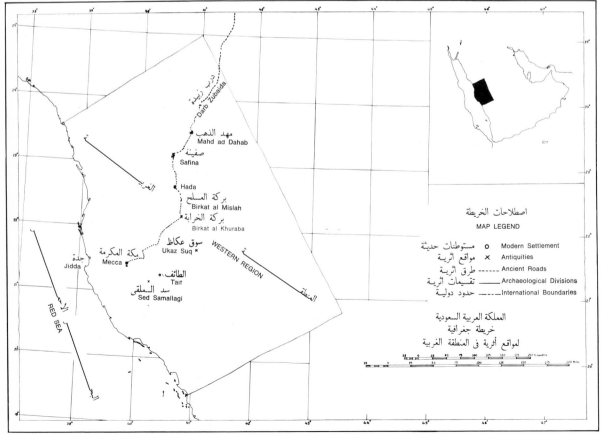

منظر جانبي لبركة الخرابة ، احدى برك درب زبيدة التاريخي الذي كان يربط بين العراق والاراضي المقدسة . وتقع هذه البركة حوالي ٩٥ كيلو مترا شمال شرقي الطائف ، و قد تم ترميمها حديثا .

Birkat al-Khuraba, 95 km. NE of Taif, one of the pools along the Darb Zubaida, or Pilgrims' Road, built by Zubaida, wife of Harun ar-Rashid, an Abbasid caliph (c. 806 A.D.). The pool, which has been recently restored, is 6 m. in depth and c. 40 m. in diameter, with 21 steps leading down into it.

اصطلاحات الخريطة
MAP LEGEND

o مستوطنات حديثة	Modern Settlement
x مواقع أثرية	Antiquities
----- طرق أثرية	Ancient Roads
——— تقسيمات أثرية	Archaeological Divisions
----- حدود دولية	International Boundaries

المملكة العربية السعودية
خريطة جغرافية
لمواقع أثرية في المنطقة الغربية

Geographical Map of the Archaeological Sites of the Western Region.

المنطقة الغربية

الحجاز

ان المنطقة الغربية من المملكة (الحجاز) تحتفظ بأهم وأعظم مآثر الأمة العربية والاسلامية جمعاء . فالى جانب الحرمين الشريفين فى مكة المكرمة والمدينة المنورة فانه يكمن بين جنباتها العديد من المواقع والأماكن التاريخيه الهامه التى سجلت ذكرى مولد الدعوة الاسلامية الخالدة والتى تشهد آثارها الباقية على عظمة التجربة التى خاضها سيد الأمة وصحبه الأجلاء فى سبيل اعلاء كلمة الله عز وجل ثم بناء الصرح الشامخ لحضارة الاسلام الزاهرة .

ففى مكة المكرمة تزخر مواقع بذكرى فجر الدعوة منها مكان مولد خاتم المرسلين ، ودار الأرقم ، ومنزل السيدة خديجة رضى الله عنها وغير ذلك الكثير . وحول مكة تشمخ قمم غار حراء وجبل النور كشواهد علياء للحدث العظيم . والمدينة المنورة تزخر بالمئات من المواقع الاسلامية الخالدة . لكل ذلك فقد كان حريا بأن ينفرد كتاب مصور خاص بآثار البقاع المقدسة ، والذى سوف يصدر قريبا باذن الله .

ومانستعرضه هنا عن آثار المنطقة الغربية هوعبارة عن لمحات موجزة لبعض الآثار المعمارية خارج الأراضى المقدسة وبالذات فى منطقة الطائف ــ والتى يرجع بعضها الى الفترة الاسلامية المبكرة . وكما هو معروف فالطائف كانت حاضرة لقبيلة ثقيف ويقع حولها الكثير من الاطلال الأثرية القديمة مثل قرية المعدن ، حوالى ٢٥ كم جنوبيها . وهناك العديد من النقوش الثمودية التى تنتشر على حواف الجبال المحيطة بالطائف ، والتى تدل على أن الثموديين كانوا السكان الأصليين لشمال غربى الجزيرة العربية .

سد السملقى : يقع هذا السد بأعلى وادى ليه ، من ضواحى مدينة الطائف ، وعلى مسافة ٣٥ كم جنوبى المدينة . وهوسد أثرى قديم من المرجح أن يكون قد تم بناؤه فى الفترة السابقة لظهور الاسلام ، ولاتزال معظم جوانبه قائمة . ويتميز السد بضخامته ــ حيث يبلغ طوله حوالى ٢٠٠ متر وعرضه ١٠ أمتار وكبر الأحجار المصقولة التى أستخدمت فيه ، وهو بلاشك يدل دلالة واضحه على تقدم فن العماره والتشييد لدى القبائل العربية التى كانت تقطن المنطقة آنذاك وقد أقيم السد فى هذا المكان بالذات بغية تحوير المياه التى تتجمع فى أعلى الوادى ولتصريفها على الحقول التى كانت قائمة على جانبيه .

موقع عكاظ : عكاظ هوأحد ــ بل أكبر ــ أسواق العرب قبل الاسلام التى كانت تقام سنويا لأغراض أدبية وتجارية وسياسية واجتماعية .

ويقع موقع عكاظ فى الحوية ، احدى الضواحى الشماليه لمدينة الطائف . ويبعد عن مطار الحوية بحوالى عشرة كيلومترات شرقا عند ملتقى وادى شرب ووادى الأخضر . وقعت فيه حرب الفجار بين قريش وهوازن سنة ٥٩٠ للميلاد وفى عكاظ بعض الأبنية الأثرية التى تعود الى العصر العباسى ويرجح انها شيدت عند بناء برك زبيدة والتى يقع بعض منها شرقى عكاظ . وقد ظلت سوق عكاظ قائمة بعد الاسلام حتى سنة ١٢٩ عندما نهبتها الخوارج الحرورية التى ظهرت مع المختار بن عوف بمكه ، فتقلص ظلها بعد ذلك .

وكان جلالة المغفور له الملك فيصل رحمه الله أول من اهتم بتعيين وتحديد مكان سوق عكاظ عندما كلف الدكتور عبد الوهاب عزام باشا رحمه الله بزيارة المنطقة والتحقيق فى موقع السوق وتاريخه ، فكتب كتابه المعروف بعنوان (عكاظ) .

وفى الآونة الأخيرة تبنت الرئاسة العامة لرعاية الشباب برئاسة صاحب السمو الملكى الأمير فيصل بن فهد بن عبد العزيز مشروعا لاحياء سوق عكاظ ، ويتم حاليا التخطيط لاقامته سنويا .

بركة الخرابة : احدى البرك الواقعة على درب زبيدة الشهير الذى يربط ما بين العراق والأراضى المقدسة . وقد بنى الطريق لراحة وسقيا الحجاج بواسطة السيدة زبيدة زوجة الخليفة العباسى هارون الرشيد . ويبلغ عدد المحطات المعروفة للدرب حوالى ٤٥ محطة يقع أربعة منها حول الطائف .

وتقع بركة الخرابة على بعد ٩٥ كم شمال شرقى الطائف . وقد شيدت على شكل دائرى ويبلغ عمقها حوالى ٦ أمتار . ويعتبر بناء البركة من أروع شواهد فن العمارة والهندسة الاسلاميه .

The northwestern region
Ancient Midian and Dedan

This region extends from the Saudi-Jordanian border in the north to Wadi Hamd (north of Medina) in the south, and from the Red Sea on the west to Harrat Khaiber and the Hufra depression on the east. It was known during Biblical times and earlier as the land of Midian. Here, Arabia's most illustrious ancient cities once thrived as strategic points along the important routes between the Peninsula and the Mediterranean littoral.

The archaeological ruins of the area include among other things gigantic rock-cut tombs, substantial settlements surrounded by impressive walls, and thousands of ancient Arabian inscriptions. The region also boasted several commercial seaports, such as the port of Hijr (modern Wedj), Maqna (present Haql), and contemporary Muwailih.

MADAIN SALEH

This well-known site was first recorded by Greek and Roman writers and geographers under the name of Hagra (Arabic al-Hijr). Classical Arab Moslem historians Al-Tabary, Al-Qasvini and Al-Balathuri identified Hijr as the capital city of the region of Midian, an appellation which was synonymous with the entire area of modern northwest Arabia, and Arab geographers such as Al-Idrisi, Al-Mogaddissi and Al-Istakhri spoke of it as the Thamudic homeland.

The history of Madain Saleh, at this point only partially known, attests to its initial foundation as a northern Minaean town, later succeeded by Thamudic and Lihyanite settlements. No precise chronology exists as to the date and/or duration of each of these apparently consecutive occupations. The first half of the 1st millennium B.C. can, however, be suggested as the general chronological framework for the earliest occupation of the site. The exact definition of this and countless other questions should naturally await a large-scale investigation of the entire area.

The monumental architectural achievements which are today the most significant feature of Madain Saleh occurred during the Nabatean occupation which followed the Lihyanite. To the Nabateans belong the magnificent rock-carved tombs and the imposing temple-like façades which adorn the cliff faces. As yet we do not know the extent of the Nabatean hegemony and/or its influence beyond northern Arabia. Their major settlement at the famous site of Petra in modern Jordan exhibits architectural achievements identical to those at Madain Saleh, only on a larger scale. Both sites testify to the existence of a sophisticated and highly-developed socio-cultural entity. The Nabatean settlement at Madain Saleh is generally dated to the 1st century B.C., and the occupation at Petra may well have been earlier.

For the greater part of the first millennium B.C., until the region fell under Ptolemic control from Egypt, the ancient indigenous Arab population effected and maintained a wide-ranging network of international trade. This pristine system of overland trade was dealt a withering blow when the Romans began to process Indian and Far Eastern trade through Egypt, thus undermining the route through northwest Arabia.

AL-ULA

Al-Ula is the modern name of the historic oasis located along Wadi Ula north of Medina, just 20 km. south of Madain Saleh. Like Madain Saleh, ancient al-Ula played a significant role in the early history of northwest Arabia. Khuraibah, in contemporary al-Ula, was the ancient capital of the kingdom of Dedan, which existed around 3000 years ago. Several inscriptions dating to the (chronologically very uncertain) Minaean period have also been found in the area of al-Ula, which may indicate settlement here even preceding the Dedanite period. Following the Dedanite period we have evidence of Lihyanite, Thamudic and probably also Nabatean settlements.

The 1968 survey made in the area by the University of London is the latest effort undertaken to date by a western scientific expedition. The results largely confirmed earlier observations made by the two Frenchmen, Jaussen and Savignac, who visited and extensively reported on the area in 1910. Main ruins in al-Ula include:
1. Rock-cut tombs to the north of the modern town
2. The site of Khuraibah (ancient Dedan) - also north of the modern town
3. Inscribed texts and graffiti associated with tombs which occur throughout the wadi, dated to the Minaean, Lihyanite, Thamudic and Nabatean periods
4. Mahlab an-Naga: a rock-cut basin probably associated with a pre-Islamic event described in the Quran

TAIMA

The antiquities in the area of Taima rank among the earliest and most significant in northwestern Arabia. Within and along the peripheries of this historic oasis settlement lie monumental sites and thousands of inscriptions. The most prolific area in this regard is located atop the important Jebel Ghunaim, 10 km. SE of the oasis. Historic Taima enjoyed a strategic position with respect to the trade routes connecting the holy places in the Hejaz with the Mediterranean littoral. Additional routes connected it with southern Iraq, the rest of the northwest, and Egypt. The Thamudic inscriptions from Taima, dubbed by Winnett and Reed the Taimanite Thamudic, are of the earliest type known.

By far the greatest fame of Taima rests, however, in its identification as the place of sojourn of Nabonidus, the last king of the Neo-Babylonians. Some of the palaces reputed to have been built by him may be lying beneath the vast ruins and tells which mass within the great wall surrounding the settlement of ancient Taima. An inscription ascribed to the king himself, found at Harran in Turkey, relates the details of Nabonidus' flight to and residence in Taima. "I hied myself afar from my city of Babylon (on) the road to Tema', Dadanu ..." He apparently overthrew the local ruler (**malku**) and took over Taima. "He made the town beautiful, built (there) his palace like the palace in (Babylon)."

One of the most distinguished ruins inside present Taima is Bir Haddaj, an ancient well where the famous Taima Stone (now at the Louvre) was found by Huber in 1884. The stone bears an important religious inscription written in ancient Aramaic.

QURAYYAH

Qurayyah is one of the most important archaeological sites in northwestern Saudi Arabia. Its significance derives both from its considerable size and from the succession of early periods of settlement represented there. The site lies 70 km. NW of the modern city of Tabuk. The first western explorer to visit and report on it was B. Moritz in 1906, and it was also later described by Philby. Among the principal ruins in the Qurayyah area are:

1. Two impressive enclosure walls on the summit of an isolated one kilometer-long citadel tell crowned with several fortifications
2. A large irregularly-shaped settlement located below the citadel, also surrounded by a wall
3. Inscriptions and graffiti associated with tombs of the Thamudic and Nabatean periods
4. Qanat-like irrigation ditches

AL-BIDA

The ruins of Maghair Shuaib lie at the end of the Wadi Al-Abiadh (now known as Wadi Afal) and on the eastern coast of the Gulf of Aqaba. The author of **The Periplus of the Erithrean Sea** (c. 1st century B.C.) referred to the inhabitants of this area as the people of "Bethmuni", who were settled in the large oasis historically known as Uyaynah. Elsewhere along Wadi Afal are several substantial ruins. Chief among them are the Nabatean tombs, some of which bear Lihyanite, as well as Nabatean, inscriptions.

Among the earliest western travellers who visited the al-Bida area were Musil and Philby. They recorded several Nabatean ruins at locations known as Hawra and Malqat. In 1968 the University of London survey confirmed these observations.

A Latin text removed from the wall of a local house, probably in Hawra, records the fact that some of the settlements were founded during the Nabatean-Roman period. The modern port city at al-Haql, 40 km. NE of al-Bida, is known to be the ancient port of Maqna.

RAWWAFAH

The site of Rawwafah lies on the trade route which connected NW Arabia with the Levant in Nabatean times. Its most impressive ruin is the precisely-dated Nabatean-Roman temple built between 166-169 A.D., nearly half a century after the collapse of the Nabatean kingdom. No evidence of actual occupation or settlement exists at this site. Its probable function was that of a way station, situated as it was on the historically well-known route leading into Jordan and the Levant through the Wadi Rumm.

واجهات ثلاثة أضرحة نحتت على الناحية الغربية من «قصر البنت» . نموذج البناء المتدرج أعلا الواجهات يعتبر أحد ظواهر العمارة النبطية في العهد الأخير .

Three major tomb façades carved into the west face of Qasr al-Bint. Note the upper parts of the façades which bear the inverted step-pyramid design, a distinctive feature of Nabatean tomb architecture.

تفصيل لواجهة ضريح فى «قصر البنت» نحتت عليها رسوم وثعابين تحيط بقناع ، و نجوم دائرية .

Detail of a west-facing tomb at Qasr al-Bint: tomb pediment adorned with a mask and two snakes and, above the architrave, a frieze of triglyphs and rosettes.

نقش نبطى يعلو واجهة أحد معابد «قصر البنت» ويحمل اسم صاحب الضريح وتاريخ وفاته .

The *tabula ansata* (framed and re-cessed panel containing the in-scription stating the name of the deceased and the year of his death) of a tomb at Qasr al-Bint.

داخل أحد أضرحة «قصر البنت» ، وتظهر فتحات المدافن ومدخل مدفن آخر يسار الصوره .

Interior of a tomb at Qasr al-Bint showing burial slots and an alcove and, to the left, a door to an inner tomb.

منظر تفصيلى لواجهة ضريح مرتفع فى «قصر البنت» .

Prominant tomb façade on the west face of Qasr al-Bint.

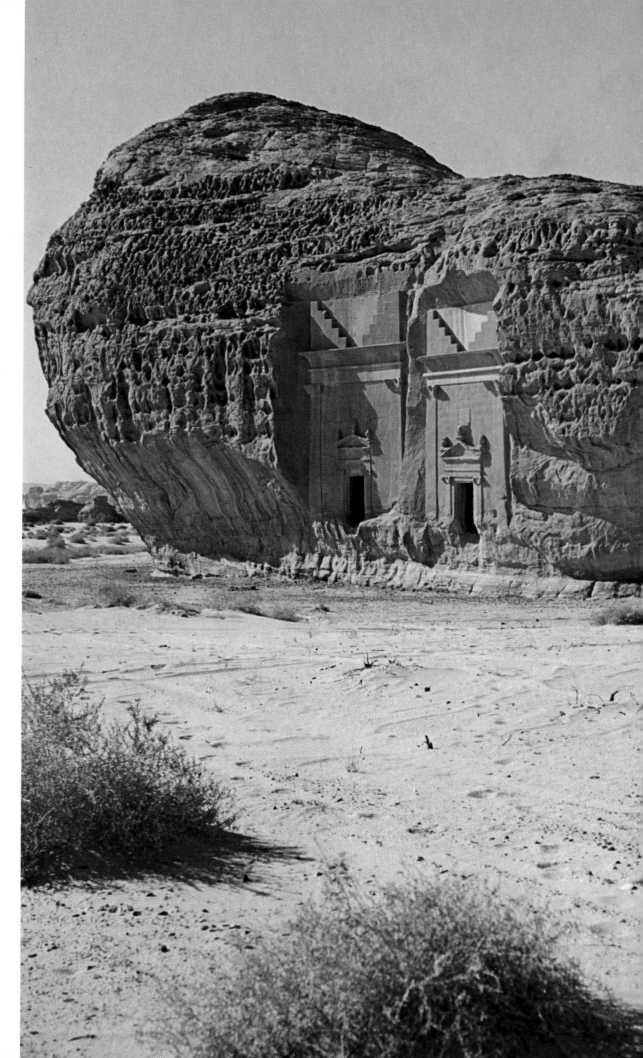

واجهتا ضريحين فى «خريبه» بمدائن صالح ، ويلاحظ أثر عوامل التعريه فى تشكيل واجهة الصخر الطبيعى .

Two west-facing tombs at Hreba, a smaller outcrop at Madain Saleh, containing 13 tombs. The doorways have been eroded to a position c. 3 m. above the present ground surface.

Majlis as-Sultan, a huge room hol-
lowed out of solid rock at Madain
Saleh. The room is 40 ft. square
and 25 ft. high and is considered
to have been a Nabatean sanctuary. To the left can be seen the
opening of a narrow defile, resembling the *siq* at Petra, the
walls of which are carved with
many "Dushara niches", Dushara
being the chief god of the Nabateans.

تفصيل الكوات المنحوته على جانب المعبر
المؤدى الى «مجلس السلطان» (انظر الصورة
المقابلة) .

Details of two "Dushara niches":
Typical Nabatean eagle and urns
Three *betyls*, or upright stones, the
central one probably representing
Dushara, perhaps flanked by con-
sorts, Manatu and Allat.

منظر عام للمعبر المؤدى الى «مجلس السلطان»
وقد نحتت على جانبه كوات أخرى لتكريم
المعبود الوثني ذو الشرى .

General interior view of defile looking west, showing the position
of two "Dushara niches" on the
left wall-face. Both depict a single
upright *betyl* (Dushara?).

Uncompleted tomb façade in the
southern part of Hremat.

تفصيل لواجهة ضريح صغير فى«حريمات»
تظهر عليه نحت قناع و نجوم دائرية .

Detail of a minor tomb façade at
Hremat embellished with a mask
and two rosettes and a row of
step-pyramids in low relief.

واجهتا ضريحين فى «حريمات» بمدائن صالح .

Two major tombs at Hremat, a
conglomeration of intricately eroded sandstone outcrops on the west
side of Madain Saleh. The elabo-
rate tomb on the left is adorned
with a double row of pilasters.

نقوش و مخربشات ثمودية على سفح جبل
بالقرب من «حريمات» فى مدائن صالح .

Thamudic inscriptions and graffiti
on a jebel face near Hremat, depicting monkey-like animals.

منظر جبل فى مدائن صالح نحت عليه
قناة لجلب مياه الأمطار الى مدخل الضريح
أسفله . (على الصفحة التالية)

preceding page
Outcrop at Madain Saleh exhibiting a man-made water conduit
carved in the rock face. Designed
to catch winter rain water, it emp-
ties into a chamber at the bottom
of the outcrop.

تفصيل لتاج عمود نبطى يعلو واجهة أحد
أضرحة حريمات .

Detail of a typical Nabatean pilas-
ter captial on a tomb at Hremat.

ضريح مهدم من جراء الانهيار الطبيعى
للصخور .

A partially destroyed tomb on the
southern face of Qasr al-Bint.

تفصيل الأفريز على واجهة ضريح في «قصر البنت» ، مزدانا بنحت أبو الهول والنجوم الدائرية .

Detail of a frieze embellished with triglyphs, rosettes, and a sphinx at Qasr al-Bint.

منظر ضريحين صغيرين من الفئة القديمة في مدائن صالح .

Two minor tomb façades at Hremat, illustrating the simpler early type of Nabatean tomb.

شاهد قبر عثر عليه فى منطقة العلا ــ
مدائن صالح ، نحت عليه شكل تجريدى
لانسان بلباس الحزام .

Stone grave marker found in the
northwest area which can probably be attributed to either al-Ula
or Taima.

داخل ضريح فى مدائن صالح يوضح الأشكال
المستطيلة للمدافن .

Tomb interior at Madain Saleh,
showing rectangular burial slots.

أضرحة العلا : منظر تفصيلي .

Al-Ula: general view, including the two lion tombs in left center.

منظر تفصيلي لأحد الحجرات المنحوته أسفل أضرحة العلا الموضحة أعلاه .

Closeup of a large chamber tomb at al-Ula.

المظهر الخلفي لأحد التماثيل في العلا والتي عثر عليها في المعبد اللحياني قرب «الخريبة» ، ويبلغ طوله حوالي المتر .

Rear view of a statue of red sandstone, measuring slightly over a meter in height, from the Lihyanite sanctuary at al-Khuraibah in al-Ula.

العلا : منظر يشمل أطلال «الخريبة» فى المقدمة ، جزء من واحة العلا فى الوسط وجبال العلا الشامخة فى المؤخرة .

Al-Ula Oasis, with the ruins of al-Khuraibah in the foreground, and the palm trees of modern al-Ula appearing against a background of towering sandstone cliffs.

واجهة تمثال العلا الذى وجد فى المعبد اللحيانى .

Front view of Lihyanite statue illustrated on pag. 63.

محلب الناقة فى العلا : حوض منحوت من الصخر يبلغ قطره ٤ أمتار ويزيد عمقه عن مترين . وربما كان له علاقة بقصة سيدنا صالح التى جاء ذكرها فى القرآن الكريم .

Mahlab an-Nagah, an ancient water tank, probably associated with the Lihyanite sanctuary at al-Khuraibah. The tank is approximately 4 meters in diameter and 2.5 meters in depth.

قلعة موسى بن نصير تعلو قمة جبل موسى
فى العلا .

The remains of Qalat Musa bin
Nusair crown the crest and sheer
forbidding slopes of this jebel at
al-Ula. It is reputed to have been
built by the famous Moslem general who achieved the conquest
of North Africa and Spain during
the Umayyid Period (c. 7th century A.D.).

الجزء الأعلى من تمثال حجرى وجد فى
المعبد اللحيانى «بخريبة» العلا .

Red sandstone torso of a statue
from the Lihyanite sanctuary at
al-Ula.

شاهد قبر من تيماء : يعود تاريخه الى
القرن الخامس ق . م ـ

Grave marker from Taima. Mid-
first millennium B.C.

العلا : مسلة لحيانية ، طولها حوالى المتر
كتب عليها بالخط اللحيانى الذى يعود
تاريخه الى القرن الثالث ق . م .
ويذكر النقش اسماء عبدة ذوغبت .

Inscribed stele from al-Ula, over
a meter in height. The inscription
mentions the names of a family of
worshippers of the Lihyanite deity,
Thu Hgebbat (c. 3rd century B.C.).
(Stele is upside down).

سد الحصيد جنوب خيبر ، يرجع تاريخ بنائه
الى ماقبل الاسلام .
منظر أسفل السد .
سطح السد .
أعلا السد .
تفصيل للواجهة الداخلية من أعلا السد ،
و يتضح نموذج البناء المتدرج الشبيه بسد
السملقى قرب الطائف .

Sed al-Khasid, a pre-Islamic dam
35 km. south of Khaiber.
Downstream view.
Top view.
Upstream view.
Closeup of upstream side. Stepped
construction technique is identical
to that of Sed Samallagi, near Taif.

قصر مرحب فى خيبر : يعود أساس بنائه
الى فترة ما قبل الاسلام .

Qasr Morheb, a late pre-Islamic
castle, sits atop a rocky promon-
tory at Khaiber. ▶

اطلال أحد المبانى الاسلاميه أسفل قصر
مرحب بخيبر .

An early Islamic building in old
Khaiber, situated below Qasr Morheb. ▶

منظر شامل لأطلال المدينة القديمة في خيبر.

General view of the old town of Khaiber from Qasr Morheb.

منظر جزئى لبئر الهداج الشهيرة فى تيماء :
يحتمل أن يعود تاريخ بنائها الى القرن
الثالث ق . م . و فيها وجدت مسلةتيماء
الهامة .

Ain Haddaj, a large ancient well at Taima (c. 1000 B.C.). It was probably built at the same time as the city wall, since it exhibits the same construction technique.

تفصيل لداخل السور في تيماء وقد اندثرت بعض أجزائه تحت الرمال .

Detail of the interior of an outer wall of Qasr al-Ablaq, Taima. The building is possibly a sanctuary, built in the mid-first millennium B.C.

شاهد قبر من الحجر وجد في تيماء وعليه رسم تجريدى يمثل المعبود الوثنى هلال .

Stone grave marker from Taima depicting the Thamudic moon god, Helal, and bearing a Lihyanite/Dedanite inscription.

جزء من سورتيماء الضخم : يرجع تاريخه الى أكثر من ٢٥٠٠ سنه سابقة .

A section of the exterior of the city wall of ancient Taima, built c. 1000 B.C. The wall, constructed of roughly-shaped sandstone blocks, is preserved to a height of 4 m. in places.

قاعدة عمود حجرى من أحد أبنية قصر الأبلق (السموأل) في تيماء .

Stone column base from Qasr al-Ablaq, Taima.

منظر شامل يوضح امتداد سور تيماء والذي
يبلغ طوله أكثر من ثلاثه كيلو مترات .

The western city wall of ancient
Taima, looking north. The original
wall is presumed to have been
over 3 km. in total length.

77 - ١١٦

منظر عام لأطلال قصر الرضم في تيماء والذى
شيد أساسه قبل ٢٣٠٠ سنه سابقة .

General view of Qasr ar-Radim,
originally built in the mid-first millennium B.C., on the tell of Taima.

منظر آخر للمبانى المضافة الى قصر الرضم
وتظهر امامه بوابة ضخمة .

Later addition to Qasr ar-Radim:
detail of a doorway.

إحدى المبانى المضافة الى قصر الرضم بعد
بنائه الأصلى .

Qasr ar-Radim: wall, probably built
as a later addition. (Note differ-
ence of construction technique
from wall in opposite figure).

قصر الرضم : دعامات السور المشيد من
الحجار المصقوله .

Southern outer wall of Qasr ar-
Radim, illustrating the dry-stone
technique and use of square but-
tresses.

Graffiti and inscriptions in Taimanite Thamudic on Jebel Ghunaim overlook the site of Taima in the distance.

تجويفات منحوته فى الصخر على قمة جبل غنيم ، يعتقد انها ذات مغزى لطقس وثنى .

Several small cup-shaped depressions, connected by grooves, on the top of Jebel Ghunaim. Possibly of ritual significance.

رسوم تجريدية على قمة جبل غنيم .

Jebel Ghunaim: detail, showing several faces of the Thamudic deity, Salm.

تفصيل لنقش ثمودى على جبل غنيم وبجانبه رسم لجمل .

Detail of a personal name inscription in Taimanite Thamudic at Jebel Ghunaim.

منطار بني عطية : برج مراقبة قرب
«القرية» ويعود الى نفس التاريخ .

Mintar Beni 'Atiya, a watch-tower
located 8 km. NW of Taima, contemporary with the ancient city.

نقش ثمودي تيمائي منحوت على جدار في
منطار بني عطية .

Mintar Beni 'Atiya: detail of a wall
bearing inscriptions of three personal names in Taimanite Thamudic.

منظر جزئي لسور قلعة «القرية» القديمة
التي يرجع تاريخها الى ٣٠٠٠ سنة سابقة .

Section of the western wall of the
citadel of Qurayyah, a substantial
settlement site presumed to date
to the first millennium B.C. or
earlier.

فرن قديم لصنع الفخار ضمن اطلال مبانى «القرية» .

Pottery kiln, located at the eastern base of the citadel hill at Qurayyah.

كسر الفخار الملون الذى ينتشر على سطح موقع «القرية» .

Closeup of early painted pottery (c. 12th-10th centuries B.C.) located near the kiln illustrated above.

«القرية» : منظر شامل لأسوار القلعة .

Qurayyah: western and eastern walls of the citadel. Constructed in sections, they are similar to the city wall of Taima.

جزء من مبنى نبطى / رومانى بين أطلال «القرية» .

Corner of a building at Qurayyah, possibly a Nabatean or Roman official residence.

بقايا فخارية من المبنى النبطى / الرومانى .

Architectural fragments from the Nabatean building at left.

أطلال على شكل دائرة من الحجر فى أسفل قلعة «القرية» .

Ancient stone circle, 55 m. in diameter, at Qurayyah. Date unknown.

رسوم لاقدام انسانية نحتت على صخر فى «القريــة» .

Graffiti of human feet on the citadel hill of Qurayyah.

بئر السعيدى : يعتقد انها نبطية وتقع بالقرب من آثار البدع .

Bir Saidi, probably a Nabatean well associated with the site of al-Bida to the west.

واجهة ضريح منحوت فى الصخر بالبدع
(مغاير شعيب) ويعود الى عصر الأنباط .

Nabatean tomb featuring a double
row of step-pyramids at Maghair
Shuaib in al-Bida. (Arabic graffiti
is modern).

منظر شامل لأضرحة البدع وقد نحتت على
عدة مستويات من الجبل .

Distance view of two decorated
Nabatean tombs at Maghair Shuaib, with simpler tombs, also of
Nabatean date, located above and
to the right. (The right hand decorated tomb is illustrated in opposite figure).

مدخل لضريح نبطي .

Doorway of a Nabatean tomb, cut in natural rock.

منظر تفصيلى لأطلال معبد روافة .

Closer view of the most well-preserved portion of the Rawwafah temple.

معبد روافة : ويقع منفردا بين الجبال شمال غربي تبوك . ويعود الى الفترة النبطية ـ الرومانية حيث تم بناؤه ، بين ١٦٦ ـ ١٦٩ م .

An isolated Nabatean/Roman temple at Rawwafah, 115 km. SW of Tabuk, stands silhouetted against a backdrop of sculptured natural stone. Its construction can be precisely dated to 166-169 A.D.

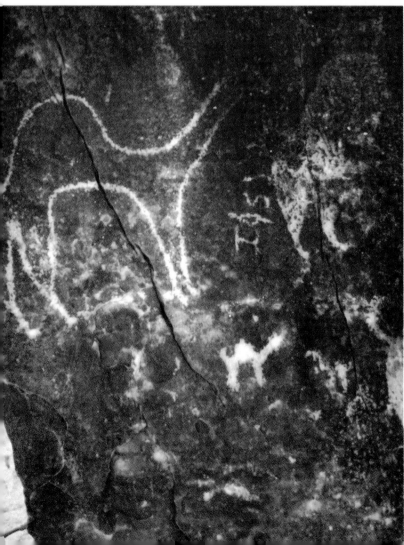

رأس تمثال لحياني وجد فى العيص قرب
ينبع النخل – يعود تاريخه الى القرن
الثالث ق ٠ م ٠

Lihyanite head of basalt from al-Is
(Yenbo) - c. 4th-3rd centuries B.C.

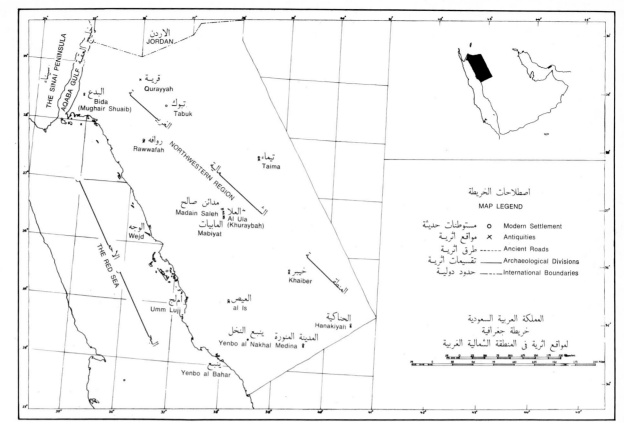

Geographical Map of Archaeological Sites of the Northwestern
Region.

ومن آثارها اليوم ما يسمى بالخبو الشرقى والخبو الغربى وغار الحمام وجبل غنيم ، وفاو الطليحة هـداج وهى بئر غزيرة المـاء عثر بها على مسلة تيماء الشهيرة المكتوبة بالخط الأرامى والمحفوظة حاليا بمتحف اللوفر بباريس ، ومن آثار تيماء أيضاً مايعرف اليوم بقصر زلوم ، وهو الأبلق المشهور فى الأدب العربى بقصر السمؤل . أما الآثار والنقوش التى عثر عليها فى قمة جبل غنيم الذى يبعد عن تيماء ٩ كم الى الجنوب الشرقى فهى تدل غاية الدلالة على انه المكان الأول والأصلى للعبادة الوثنية التى كان يعتنقها الثموديون وهى عبادة «صلم»

القرية : تقع على بعد ٧٠ كم شمال غربى تبوك ، وعلى بعد ٦٠ كم جنوبى المدورة ، وهى من اهم المناطق الأثرية بالمملكة ، وتدل آثار الرى فيها بان نظاما دقيقا للرى قد قام فى هذه المنطقة فى عهد يعود الى مطلع الألف الأول قبل الميلاد . وتوجد بها آثار مدينة كبيرة ذات ابراج وأسوار ضخمة ومقابر وكهوف مما يشير الى ان القرية ذات تاريخ عميق وحضارة موغلة فى القدم لانزال نجهل عنها الكثير .

رواقة : تقع فى قلب منطقة حسمى ، وعلى بعد ٧٤ كم غربى تبوك ، ويوجد بها بقايا معبد رومانى نبطى يعود الى القرن الثانى للميلاد حسب محتوى النقش الرومانى المؤرخ بعصر ماركوس أورليوس ، والذى عثر عليه بين انقاض المعبد . ويشبه معبد رواقة معبدا رومانيا بوادى (رم) بالأردن وكلاهما على الطريق التجارى العربى القديم .

البدع «مغاير شعيب» : يقع فى نهاية وادى الأبيض المسمى (عفاله) على الجانب الشرقى لخليج العقبة ، ويبعد عن تبوك مسافة ١٧٠ كم غربا . وتتصل به واحة فسيحة سماها بطليموس بالعيينة . وفى كل مكان داخل الوادى ومن حوله تنتشر خرائب كثيرة لمدن وقرى ، أبرزها وأحدثها المقابر النبطية التى كتب عليها من الداخل العديد من النقوش اللحيانية والنبطية ، وتعتبر تلك الخرائب المتناثرة دليل واضح على أن أمما كثيرة قد تعاقبت على سكنى الواحة ابان ازدهارها التجارى والزراعى قبل الميلاد بعدة قرون ومرفأ (الحقل) اليوم هو ميناء البدع القديم وكان يسمى (مقنا) ويقع من البدع على مسافة تقدر بأربعين كيلومترا الى الشمال الشرقى .

المنطقة الشمالية الغربية
أرض مدين ودادان

وتمتد هذه المنطقة من «المدورة» شمالا الى وادى الحمض (شمال المدينة المنورة) جنوبا ، فالحسمة شرقا فالبحر الاحمر غربا ، وكانت تعرف فى التاريخ القديم وفى الكتب المقدسة بأرض مدين . وفيها تقع أبرز مدن وآثار ما قبل الاسلام بالمملكة مثل تيماء وخيبر والعلا ومدائن صالح وقرية (بتشديد الياء) وغيرها من المناطق التى كانت تقع على الطريق التجارى القديم بين الجزيرة العربية والشام . وتكتنف آثار هذه المدن العديد من القصور والأسوار والابراج والمعابد ومئات من النقوش المعينية والدادانية واللحيانية والثمودية والنبطية .

كما تحتوى شواطىء المنطقة على عدة موانىء تجارية كان لها شأن عظيم فى التاريخ العربى القديم كميناء «الحجر» (الوجه حاليا) وميناء «مقنا» (حقل حاليا) وميناء «روافة» (المويلح حاليا) .

وقد اهتم بآثار هذه المنطقة المؤرخون العرب والغربيون خلال المائة عام السابقه ، وقد أسفرت دراساتهم الأولية على أن حضارة زاهية ، نمت وازدهرت فيها منذ حوالى ثلاثة آلاف سنة ماضية . غير أن تفاصيل تلك الحضارة لاتزال رهينة اجراء التنقيبات والبحوث الدقيقة مستقبلا .

العلا : اسم حديث لواحة تاريخية لعبت دورا هاما عندما كانت مقرا للدادانيين والمعينيين . وكان ما يسمى اليوم بالخريبة حاضرة مملكة دادان والتى تلتها دولة لحيان ثم جاء بعدها الحكم المعينى الذى انتهى باستيلاء الانباط وذلك خلال الفترة بين القرن السادس ونهاية القرن الثالث قبل الميلاد . وتقع العلا شمال المدينة المنورة فى وادى القرى بين سلسلة من الجبال فى الشرق والغرب ، ويوجد بها عدد من الأضرحة المنحوته نحتا هندسيا بارعا مع عدد من النقوش الدادانيه والمعينيه واللحيانيه والثموديه والنبطية ثم بقايا سد كان طوله ٧٥٠ مترا . ومن آثار العلا الاسلامية قلعة على قمة جبل موسى تنسب الى القائد المسلم الشهير موسى بن نصير .

مدائن صالح : تقع على مسافة ١٥ كيلومترا شمال العلا . وقد جاءت فى القرآن الكريم باسم (الحجر) كحاضرة ثمود قوم نبى الله صالح . وتشتمل المنطقة على عدة كهوف ومقابر منحوته فى الجبال الرملية المتقاربة ، وهذه المدافن كما تدل نقوشها كانت مقابر لأقوام كثيرة ممن حكموا المنطقة من أنباط ورومان وعرب ، وهى تشبه الى حد كبير مقابر (البتراء) عاصمة الانباط القديمة وتقع الآن بالأردن . وعلى واجهات المقابر تماثيل وصور ورؤس خرافية وثنية يعود نحتها الى القرن الثانى قبل الميلاد . وتوجد بالقرب من منطقة المقابر آثار مستوطنات قديما ربما كانت مساكنا لسكان مدائن صالح فى عصورها المختلفة . وقد اشتهرت عند المؤرخين اليونان والرومان بهجرا وكان لها ميناء يسمى باسمها (الوجه حاليا) وكان يعتبر شريانا تجاريا هاما .

ويظهر من تنوع آثار الحجر وفنونها المختلفة أن بدء حياة وازدهار المنطقة يعود الى ماقبل آلاف السنين اذ ظلت زمنا طويلا تتلقى تجارة الشرق القادمة بواسطة الموانئ العربية فى الجنوب وتصدرها نحو الغرب بواسطة موانئ سوريا فى الشمال ، كما يستشف من دراسة الخرائب المتناثرة فى المنطقة وحولها أن شعوبا كثيفة قد تجمعت هناك وعاشت لعدة قرون ، ولاشك أن عمليات التنقيب القادمة انشاء الله ستكشف لنا الكثير والكثير عن خبايا وتاريخ هذه الأرض .

تيماء : وتبعد مسافة ١٠٠ كيلو مترا شمال شرقى مدائن صالح ـ وهى مركز آخر من مراكز الحضارة العربية القديمة لوقوعها هى الأخرى على الطريق التجارى بين بابل ومصر ومكه والشام . وقد جاء ذكرها فى نقش تيقلاث بلاسر الثالث الملك الاشورى (٧٤٤ ـ ٧٢٧ قبل الميلاد) .

كما يحدثنا نقش نابونيدوس ملك بابل (القرن السادس عشر قبل الميلاد) الذى عثر عليه فى حوران بسوريا ان هذا الملك البابلى قد اتخذ من تيماء مأوى يحتمى به من حملات قورش الامبراطور الفارسى . وقدمكث بها عشر سنوات وبنى فيها عدة قصور .

The northern region
Jebel Shammar and Wadi As-Sirhan

The northern region includes some of the earliest cities of Arabia, such as Jouf (the biblical Dumah), Hail, and the towns of Wadi as-Sirhan. Both Assyrian and Chaldean literary evidence attest to the long and involved relationship between these urban settlements of northern Arabia and the nuclear areas of ancient civilization to the north. The inhabitants of the region were collectively known as the peoples of Adumatu and were a subject of interest, and at times, of military conquest, to the kings of Assur, Babylon and Persia.

WADI SIRHAN - QARYAT AL-MILH

This large and well-known wadi in north Arabia has always been the main access route between this region and Syria to the north. At its southern end lies the Jouf Oasis, while at its northernmost extension within the kingdom lie the group of oases settlements collectively known as **Qaryat al-Milh** ("villages of the salt"), so named because of the considerable salt deposits found in the area. The most well-known villages of this group are an-Nabk, Kaf, Manwa, al-Haditha and al-Qarqar. Main ancient ruins in the **Qaryat** include:

1. Ithra: A Nabatean palace is located within the present palm gardens of the village. The main gate of the palace (**qasr**) bears a Kufic inscription and inside a mustached face is carved on a stone. A small Nabatean sanctuary is also located outside the center of the village with an Iron Age settlement near-by.
2. Kaf: Atop a mountainous outcrop called Jebel as-Saidi are to be found remnants of an Iron Age settlement succeeded by a temple which was originally built by the Nabateans. In Islamic times the temple was reused as a mosque.
3. Al-Haditha: Near this village can be found some ancient irrigation channels, a ruin of a palace, and a cemetery, all probably dated to the end of the first millennium B.C.
4. Al-Ugailah: The foundations of at least three unusually large rectangular buildings and field walls, can be seen at this site along the modern highway between Turaif and **Qaryat al-Milh**. The cultural debris around these ruins indicate a settlement possibly dating to as early as c. 600 B.C.

SAKAKA

Sakaka is another oasis town, located to the northwest of Jouf, which now functions as the main administrative center of the area. Several historic monuments and ancient sites can be found in and around the oasis. Among these are:

1. Qasr Zabal: This irregularly-shaped fort, composed of four towers with a circular building inside, sits atop a high outcrop overlooking the oasis. It is believed to have been built less than 150 years ago.
2. Jebel Burnus: Located c. 100 ft. from Qasr Zabal, this jebel exhibits several carved rock-drawings in the shape of "dancing" figures with tasselled heads and upraised arms. The work is believed to date to pre-Islamic times.
3. Bir Sisar: This semi-rectangular well, cut into solid rock, possesses stairs carved into its northern and eastern sides and is located just 150 m. west of Qasr Zabal. Two openings of unknown purpose are cut underneath the stairs. The precise date of the well is unknown, but it is presumed to have been built in the early centuries A.D.
4. Qarah: Mountainous outcrops near this village situated 5 km. south of Sakaka are adorned with extensive Thamudic inscriptions and graffiti of c. 3rd-2nd century B.C. date.
5. Rajajil: At the base of a low-lying outcrop 7 km. south of Qarah is situated an area of ancient structures possibly dating as early as c. 2000 B.C. These structures are marked by impressive standing stone pillars, roughly carved, and arranged in linear groups aligned along a general North bearing. The pillars measure up to 3 m. in height and some of them bear early graffiti and inscriptions.

AL-JOUF

In the oasis of al-Jouf lies one of the earliest recorded ancient settlements in north Arabia. It was justly called the gateway to the area. In former times the oasis was known as **Domat al-Jandal** (literally "Domat of the Stones"), the **Dumah** mentioned in the Old Testament. Earlier still it was referred to as Adumatu by the Assyrians of the early-mid first millennium B.C. After that it can probably be identified as the town of Adummu, which was besieged c. 552 B.C. by the famous Nabonidus, the last king of the Neo-Babylonian period in Mesopotamia. This was the same Nabonidus who later took refuge at Taima, south of Jouf. Main ruins in the Jouf area include:

1. Qasr Marid (also known as Qasr al-Ukaider): This is the most impressive structure at Jouf. It is constructed of stones and mud-brick and functioned as a fortress. Its original foundation is believed to date to the 3rd century B.C.; however, it has since witnessed many rebuildings, especially during the reign of al-Ukaider as-Sukuni, a ruler of Jouf at the beginning of the Islamic Period.
2. Omar Mosque: This is an ancient stone-built mosque with a tower-like minaret located near Qasr Marid. The foundations of the structure are believed to date to the reign of the Caliph Omar (634-644 A.D.), with several successive additions dating to later times.
3. Minaean inscribed stones: The Minaean inscription found at Jouf are among the rarest such inscriptions found in north Arabia, since Minaean is very much confined to south Arabia.

HAIL

Hail is presently the principal city in central north Arabia, a position which it held in late historic times as well. It is located among large mountainous outcrops which collectively comprise the well-known Jebel Shammar area. In recent and late historic times Hail was a town of some strategic importance in the region. It represented the political and cultural center of the Shammar area.

Its earlier identity is somewhat in doubt. As early as the late 19th century western scholars suggested its equation with the **Arre Kome** or **Aine** of Ptolemy (2nd century A.D.). It is also believed that through ancient Hail ran the trade route which connected the famed, but so far unlocated, ancient emporium of Gerrha on the Arabian Gulf with the Levant coast. Known archaeological sites in and around Hail include:

1. Qasr ibn Rashid: Located in the city itself, this is one of Hail's oldest and most picturesque fort-palaces, built around the latter part of the 19th century A.D. It is distinguished by elegantly painted rooms with finely-carved and painted doors and windows (now torn down).
2. Fayd: The site contains ruins of pre-Islamic buildings constructed of the native basalt which is the result of ancient volcanic activity in the area. Early Arab tradition refers to Fayd as the oldest settlement in the northern Nejd area of central Arabia, probably dating from 3000-2500 years ago.
3. Jebel Salma: Inscriptions and graffiti here have been identified as mainly Thamudic inscriptions of the Nejdi type, extending back to as early as 2600 years ago.
4. Samira (Jebel Aja area, northwest of Hail): This site is reputed to be the original settlement of the Tayy tribal group, renowned for their poetic lore and extreme generosity, both during the pre-Islamic and Islamic periods.
5. Jebel Yatib: This jebel abounds with inscribed texts of Thamudic and Palmyrene, as well as Islamic Arabic, origin. In addition to the texts, graffiti and several pictorial representations of palm trees and human figures occur. A settlement of considerable size lies immediately below the jebel. From surface indications this appears to be of early pre-Islamic date, possibly belonging to the Bronze Age.
6. Al-Shimli, Sarra and As-Siffin: These are all sites containing inscriptions, graffiti and ruins in the Jebel Aja complex.

أحد الأبواب المزخرفة من قصر بن رشيد فى حائل .

Carved and painted doorway of the 19th-century palace of Mohammed ibn Rashid at Hail.

اطلال بناء قديم يمتد طوله لأكثر من كيلومتر ، يقع غرب جبل الصعيدى بالقرب من الكاف .

Ancient stone foundations of field walls over a kilometer in length west of Jebel Saidi near Kaf, of Iron Age date.
(This, and following photos of antiquities at Kaf and Ithra are all located in the *Qaryat al-Milh* oases along Wadi Sirhan.)

منظر شامل لواحة الكاف فى «قريات الملح» ويظهر حصن الروله يسار الصورة و «قصر الصعيدى» على قمة الجبل .

General view of Kaf Oasis. Left background: Rwallah Tribe fortress. Right background: Jebel as-Saidi, crowned by Qasr as-Saidi. Both date to the late 19th century, but include Iron Age and Nabatean remains.

جانب داخلى من «قصر الصعيدى» وعـليـه كتابات عربيـة حـديثة .

Detail of stones of the gateway of Qasr as-Saidi, with a recent Arabic inscription.

منظر تفصيلى لاحدى حجرات «قصر الصعيدى» الذى شيد قبل ١٥٠ سنه فقط .

Interior view of gateway of Qasr as-Saidi.

رسمان قديمان لوعلين على جبل بالقرب من «اثرا» - قريات الملح .

Elegant graffiti of two wild goats on a basaltic outcrop near Ithra.

اثرا ـ قريات الملح : المدخل الرئيسى للقصر
النبطى ذو الطابقين والذى يعود الى القرن
الاول ق . م .

Main entrance of a large two-story
Nabatean building at Ithra Oasis,
known as Qasr Mohammed (c. 1st
century B.C.).

منظر تفصيلى لمداخل القصر النبطى وتتضح
فيه بقايا السقف .

Interior of building, illustrating the
two-story construction technique.

منظر شامل لقلعة الرولا التاريخية بالكاف
والتى تعود الى أوائل القرن الهجرى الحالى .

Panoramic view of the fortress-
palace of Nuri ibn Shaalan, para-
mount sheikh of the Rwallah tribe.

مناظر تفصيلية للقصر النبطي في اثرا
«بقريات الملح» :
البوابة الرئيسية وعليها رسوم معينية ـ سبئية
ونقش بالكوفي .
واجهة داخلية حفر عليها وجه انسان ذو
شوارب .
تفصيل للبناء المحكم .
تفصيل لبناء السقف.

Details of the Nabatean building
at Ithra:
Main gateway, decorated with
Thamudic and Arabic graffiti.
An interior façade, bearing a mustached face carved in low relief.
Two views of Nabatean construction technique in the interior. Note
unusual shapes of stones in both
figures.
Stone beams used in construction
of the roof.

Stone pillars of Rajajil, located
south of Sakaka. These were
originally vertical stone markers
for rectangular or circular stone
structures, now fallen into this
striking pattern. The pillars are
3 m. high and date to the Bronze
Age.

نقوش ومخربشات حفرت على « اعمدة
الرجاجيل » .

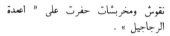

Closeup of some of the leaning
pillars, inscribed with later graffiti.

سكاكا : منظر عام يبين قصر زعبل وجزء من
الرسوم على جبل برنس (يسار الصورة) .

Sakaka: Right - general view of
Zabal fortress, of recent historic
date. Left foreground - graffiti on
Jebel Burnus.

Sisar well at Sakaka, illustrating typical Nabatean construction and featuring a staircase cut into the sides.

صورة لبغل على ظهره هودج حفرت على جبل برنس .

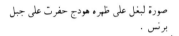

Graffiti of donkey wearing a saddle on a jebel north of Jebel Burnus.

منظر تفصيلى لقلعة زعبل فى سكاكا ، شيدت قبل حوالى ١٣٠ سنة .

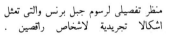

Closer view of Zabal fortress, Sakaka.

منظر تفصيلى لرسوم جبل برنس والتى تمثل اشكالا تجريدية لاشخاص راقصين .

Detail of graffiti on Jebel Burnus, depicting "dancing" figures.

الجوف «دومة الجندل» : منظر شامل يوضح قصر مارد والواحة الحالية اسفله . (على الصفحة السابقة)

overleaf
Panoramic view of Qasr Marid (also known as Ukhaider) and the oasis of Jouf (ancient Domat al-Jandal). The foundations of the *qasr* are presumed to date to 300 B.C., but the superstructure is early Islamic.

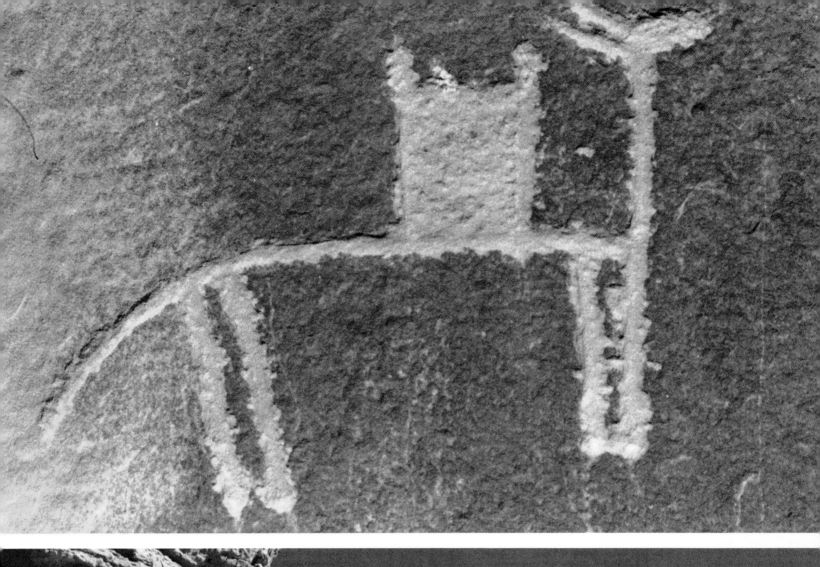

منظر تفصيلي لقصر مارد (والمعروف بالاكيدر) ، يرجع اساس بنائه الى القرن الثالث ق . م .

Closer view of an outer wall and tower of Qasr Marid.

مئذنة ومسجد عمر بالجوف وقد شيدت بأكملها من الحجر ، ينسب بناؤها الى عهد الخليفة عمر بن الخطاب رضى الله عنه .

Omar Mosque at al-Jouf, the foundations of which are attributed to the Caliph Omar (634-644 A.D.).

منظر عام يوضح موقع مسجد عمر وما حوله من
الاطلال فى واحة الجوف .

Another view of the tower of Omar
Mosque, seen amid the ruins of
the old city of Jouf.

منظر من داخل قصر مارد وتبدو بقايا جدار
مرتفع ، على يمين الصوره .

Interior view of Qasr Marid. Note
the great height to which the outer
wall on the right is preserved.

قصر مارد : منظر لبقايا المبانى التى انشئت
خلال فترات متعاقبة ، من جملتها برج من
الطين .

View from Qasr Marid toward later
additions to the structure, including a later tower.

Qalat Aarif, an Ottoman period fortress built on a prominent ridge
at Hail in 1895 A.D. or earlier.

قصر ابن رشيد بحائل : شيد في اوائل القرن
الهجري الحالي .

Qasr Mohammed ibn Rashid at
Hail, built in 1893 A.D.: general
view of interior buildings and
towers.

قصر ابن رشيد : مناظر داخلية .

Two views of the interior of Qasr
ibn Rashid. Lower figure shows a
staircase and a courtyard with
painted doors.

قصر ابن رشيد : باب خشبي مزخرف يمثل
طراز الصناعه التقليدية المتقنة .

Detail of an elaborately carved
and painted door of Qasr ibn Rashid. Note ingenious wooden lock
and key.

زخارف هندسية ملونة على احد حوائط قصر
ابن رشيد التاريخي بحائل .

Elegantly painted Islamic border
decorating the wall of a room in
the same palace with a religious
inscription atop the doorway.

زخارف ورسوم طبيعية قديمة حفرت على
جبل المليحية بالقرب من حائل ، وقد ظهرت
معها نقوش بالثمودية تعود الى القرن الثالث
ق . م .

A more ancient form of Arabian
decoration at al-Milihiya, 40 km.
SE of Hail. The inscription refers
to Thamudic deities and depicts
totemic plants and animals.

قصر حاتم الطائى : يقع شمال غربى حائل فى
قرية توران حيث سكنت قبيلة طى تاريخيا .

Qasr Hatim at-Ta'i, located 50 km.
NW of Hail and reputed to be the
palace of a famous Arab figure of
the 6th century A.D. Stone foundations underlie a superstructure
of mud-brick.

اطلال مبانى وآثار قنوات قديمة فى السفن
بالقرب من جبل أجا شمال حائل .

Safan: remnants of a pre-Islamic
structure associated with irrigation
works in a wadi adjoining Jebel
Aja, 35 km. NW of Hail.

بقايا قصر ضخم مشيد من الطوب يقع شمال
المدينة ، يحتمل أنه بنى قبل ١٥٠ سنة .

Ruins of a large palace-like structure of baked mud-brick at Milei-
leeh, 50 km. north of Medina. Reported to have been built about
155 years ago.

جبل ياطب ، حائل : منظر لرسومات عديدة
حفرت فى الصخر تمثل صورا لجمال ونخلة
وأسد تتوسطها نقوش ثمودية ـ نجدية يعود
تاريخها الى حوالى القرن الرابع ق . م .
(منظر الصفحة السابقة)

overleaf
Graffiti of palm trees, camels and
lions (?) interspersed with inscriptions in Nejdi Thamudic on Jebel
Yatib, 35 km. SE of Hail.

منظران يوضحان بعض النقوش والرسوم
الاخرى بجبل ياطب .

Two more views of graffiti-covered
rocks at Jebel Yatib.

اطلال حوض تجميع المياه المتصل باحدى
برك درب زبيدة فى منطقة فيد جنوبى حائل .

A settling basin of a Darb Zubaida
pool at Fayd, 120 km. SE of Hail,
now completely filled in with sand
and debris.

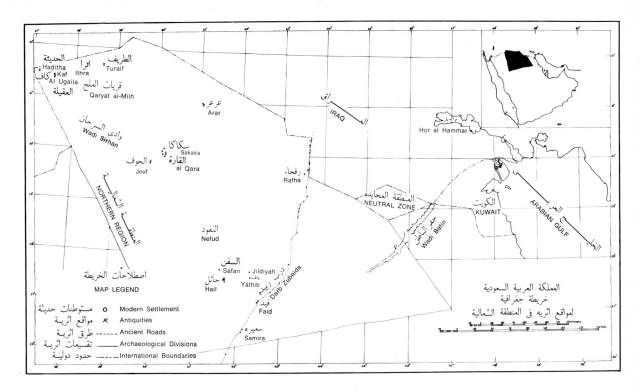

بئر سيسر : أيضا على مقربة من قصر زعبل ، وهى بئر منحوته فى الصخر ، شيدت على أحد جوانبها درج من الصخر نفسه ، وفى أسفلها توجد فتحه مستطيله تلوها فتحه أكبر لايعرف الغرض منهما .

القـارة : قرية تبعد مسافة ٥ كيلومترات جنوب سكاكا بها عدد من النقوش الثموديه ورسوم حيوانيه غريبة الأشكال .

أعمدة الرجاجيل : مجموعات من الأعمدة الحجرية يتراوح طولها بين مترين وثلاثة أمتار وضعت بشكل عمودى ، كل أربعة فى مجموعة ، كشواهد لمايعتقد أن يكون أضرحة تعود الى فترة ما قبل الميلاد .

وتقع هذه عند سفح جبل صغير يبعد مسافة سبعة كيلومترات جنوب القارة فى مكان يسمى «محمد سلطان المدارة» . وعلى أحد الأعمدة وجدت بعض النقوش الثمودية .

وادى السـرحان

عباره عن شبه واحه تبتدىء من مسافة ٢٠٠ كيلومترا شمال غربى الجوف وتنتهى شمالا فى بصرا بسوريا . وكان الوادى ، ولايزال يشكل طريقا تجاريا هاما ويعتبر المدخل الشمالى الرئيسى لجزيرة العرب ، وتنتشر فى وسطه عدة قرى صغيرة تعرف بقريات الملح والتى يستحضر فيها الملح على مصطلحات تملأ بالماء ثم تجفف وتجمع تمهيدا للتصدير .

ومن أشهر القرى : كاف ، منوه ، القرقر ، الحديثة ، النبك ، واثرا .

العقيلة : تبعد حوالى ٢٥ كم عن النبك وبها آثار أساسات لمبانى قديمة ، بالاضافه الى اطلال بنيان على شكل مستطيل يبلغ طول جداره مايزيد على كيلومترا .

كـاف : بالقرب من العقيله ، وقرب سفح جبل الصعيدى الذى بنيت عليه ،حامية لطريق الحجاج خلال العصر العباسى . ويوجد فى الكاف قصر داخل حصن كبير ينسب بناؤه الى الشيخ نورى الشعلان رئيس قبيلة الروله فى أوائل هذا القرن .

إثـره : توجد بها مبانى وآثار تعود الى الفترة النبطية . وأهمها المبنى الذى يدعى قصر محمد بن سلطان ، وهو عباره عن قصر نبطى متكامل كان لايزال تحت الاستعمال حتى زمن قريب .

للوادى الذى تقعفيه لوقوعه حائلا بين جبلى شمر ، أجا وسلمى وأنها كانت تسمى بقرية حائل ، وأخيرا أزيل اسم القرية وبقى (حائل) .

لقد كانت حائل مركزا تجاريا يربط بين طرق أربع هى : حائل ـ الجوف ، حائل ـ بريده ، حائل ـ النجف ، حائل ـ الجرعاء (على الخليج العربى) .

أشهر أماكنها الأثرية :

فيـد : وتقع على بعد ١٢٠ كم جنوبى شرق حائل وبها مايسمى خرائب «قصر خراش» الذى يعتقد أن يكون موقع مدينة قديمة تعود الى ماقبل الاسلام . وكان طريق الحج «درب زبيدة» يمربقرية فيد حيث توجد بالقرب منها بقايا لبعض البرك والمنشآت المعماريه المتعلقة بذلك المشروع الاسلامى الضخم .

جبل المليحية : يبعد عن حائل مسافة ٤٠ كم شرقا . توجد على واجهات صخوره نقوش ورسومات هامة تمثل مناظر حيه للأبقار والجمال البريه والنعام والأسود الخ .... مما يدل على تواجد كثيف لهذه الحيوانات فى الفترات السابقة .

السفن (بكسر وتشديد السين) : ويقع فى واد صغير فى سفح جبل أجا شمال غرب حائل وأهم آثاره أحواض وقنوات مائية قديمه شيدت لتصريف مياه الوادى وسقيا المزارع . ويستدل من النقوش الموجوده على جبل أجا أن الموقع قد يعود تاريخه الى ٢٥٠٠ سنه سابقه .

قصر حاتم الطائى : ويوجد بقريه توارن على سفح جبل اجا . ومن المعروف أن قبيلة طى القديمه كانت تقطن المنطقة منذ عصر ما قبل الاسلام أما نسبة القصر الى حاتم الطائى فهو أمر غير مؤكد ، وعلى أى حال فالقصر شهد فترات بناء متعاقبة حسبما يظهر من البقايا المعماريه . وبالاضافة الى هذه المواقع الرئيسيه يوجد حول حائل عدد من الجبال التى تحمل نقوشا ورسوما ثمودية نجدية والتى يرجح أن تاريخها يعود الى القرن الثالث أو الرابع لما قبل الميلاد ومن أمثال هذه ياطب جانين والشملى سراء .

قصر ابن رشيد : أحد القصور التاريخيه فى حائل والذى يرجع تاريخ بنائه الى أوائل القرن الهجرى الحالى . ومن أبرز معالمه الأبواب الخشبية المزخرفة والرسوم الهندسية التى تزين داخل بعض الحجرات .

الجـــــوف :

هوما كان يعرف قديما بدومة الجندل ، وتقع على حافة النفود الشمالى . وكانت مقرا لملوك الشعب الادومى الذى أطلق الآشوريين عليه وعلى المنطقة مسمى «أدوماتو» .

ومن آثار الجوف البارزة معقلها الحصين الذى عرف بقصر مارد أوالاكيدر والذى يعتقد أنه بنى أولا فى فترة تسبق القرن الثالث لما قبل الميلاد ، وتعاقبت عليه فترات بناء متعددة بعد ذلك . وبجانب الحصن يوجد مسجد ذو مئذنة حجرية ينسب بناؤه الى عهد الخليفة عمر بن الخطاب رضى الله عنه . وقد عثر بقصر مارد ، وغيره من المناطق الأثرية فى واحة الجوف ، على العديد من النقوش المعينية والثمودية واللحيانية والنبطية .

وكان يحكم دومة الجندل أبان بعثة الرسول ، صلى الله عليه وسلم ، الاكيدر بن عبد الملك السكونى وهو عربى من قبيلة كندة الجنوبية . وكان بدومة الجندل سوق عربية شهيرة تبدأ فى أول يوم من شهر ربيع الأول وتنتهى فى منتصفه من كل عام .

سكاكا :

قصر زعبل : مرتفع خارج سكاكا ، وهو حصن على قمة هضبة جبليه تشرف على الواحه أدناها ، ويعتقد أنه بنى منذ ١٢٠ سنه فقط .

جبل برنس : غرب قصر زعبل مباشرة وتوجد عليه رسوم لأشخاص فى مشهد راقص ، بجانبها نقوش شبيهه بالنبطيه وتختلط بها كتابات عربية .

وتشمل هذه المنطقة أقدم مدن الجزيرة العربية تاريخا كالجوف (دومة الجندل) ووادى سكاكا وقرى وادى السرحان، تلك التى عاصرت دول الآشوريين والكلدانيــين اللذين جاءت نقوشهم حاملة اسماء ملوك وشعب كان يسمى «أدوماتو» وقد كان لذلك الشعب ، على مايبدو ، مواقف بطولية فى صد غارات ملوك آشور وبابل والفرس حينما قاموا بغزواتهم العديدة على شمال الجزيرة العربية عبر النفوذ ، وتشمل المنطقة أيضا حائل وما حولها من مرتفعات جبل شمر حيث التقى شمال الجزيرة بجنوبها والتحم شرقها بالغرب .

حائـــــل :

تقع على سفح الطرف الشمالى الشرقى لجبل أجا ، وعلى بعد خمسين كيلومترا الى جنوبها الشرقى يقع جبل سلمى . وتبعد عن الرياض شمالا مسافة ٧٤٥ كيلومترا . وتقول المصادر التاريخيه أن حائلا هوالاسم الأصلى

The eastern region
Hasa and Qatif Oases

We know relatively more about the chronology of human settlement in the eastern region of the king-dom than about that of any other area. Several factors are responsible for this, not least among them being the strategic location of this region **vis-a-vis** the early centers of civilization to its north and east. Accumulating archaeological evidence points to the probability that eastern Arabia played a decisive role in cross-cultural contacts during the third millennium B.C., a period in which civilizational growth in Mesopotamia and points east was at its height. Overlooking nearly 700 km. of coastline along the Arabian Gulf (the busiest inland sea in ancient times), eastern Arabia could well have controlled a far-flung traffic in trade among the civilizations which existed 5000 years ago.

TARUT

This small island off the coast of Qatif Oasis has provided the most substantial evidence of Arabian involvement in third millennium B.C. trade. The island appears to have boasted a very active seaport which was involved in a widespread trading network. It could also have served a vital function as a link between the mainland and the flow of trade. Tarut's two traditional harbors, Sanabis, in the northeast, and Darin, in the south, both contain evidence of ancient settlements. There are, in addition, strong indications that Tarut (and perhaps also the mainland of eastern Arabia) were closely associated with the famous land of Dilmun, a large center of which has been discovered on the island of Bahrain.

STONE AGE

The semi-desertic landscape of eastern Arabia is interspersed with large productive oases. Numerous archaeological sites are associated with these, with evidence of occupation beginning in early Paleolithic times. Jabrin, the southernmost oasis, lies close to the periphery of the Empty Quarter. Just outside it, early Paleolithic occupation can be found on the tops of natural rocky outcrops. (These outcrops also served as sources of flint, utilized for the manufacture of chipped stone tools.) Large, crude handaxes and cleaver-like implements, known to be some of the earliest types of stone tools fashioned by man, are the most common artifacts found on these sites. In close proximity to the Paleolithic sites are found settlements of the later Neolithic period. The tool assemblages on these sites feature large inventories of finely-made artifacts such as arrowheads, blades, scrapers, etc.

UBAID SITES

In the succeeding chronological period (7000-6000 years ago) we find the initial evidence in eastern Arabia of direct contact with Mesopotamia. This occurred during the Ubaid Period, contemporary with the earliest-documented occupation of southern Mesopotamia. Examples of sites containing artifactual assemblages identical to Ubaid sites in Mesopotamia occur in substantial numbers in and around the major oases of eastern Arabia. Major examples of these are: Ain Qannas, 20 km. north of Hofuf; Dosariyya, on the coast 50 km. north of Hofuf; and Abu Khamis, 60 km. north along the coast from

Dosariyya. Thereafter, the degree of relationship between the two areas increased through time, until, as we have seen above, it assumed a very intensified character around 5000 years ago, when true urban civilization was beginning to flourish in the Near East.

Elsewhere in the eastern region (including the interior areas) several sites are known which exhibit characteristics that clearly distinguish them as the remains of large complex settlements. This gives us an impression of the high calibre of contact which must have brought the region into direct interaction with Mesopotamia, southwest Iran, the southern reaches of the Arabian Gulf and the Indus Valley during the third, second, and first millennia B.C.

SELEUCID PERIOD

In the latter part of the first millennium B.C., the eastern region was under extensive Greek occupation, corresponding to the Seleucid era in Mesopotamia. Large urban trading centers existed in this era, the principal ones being Thaj and Gerrha. Thaj is now a modern village located to the NW of Qatif Oasis, c. 70 km. west of the coast of the Arabian Gulf. In and around the village lie the impressive ruins of a walled Hellenistic city (c. 1st century B.C.-3rd century A.D.). The city, which thrived until late pre-Islamic times, was a major emporium along the inland route connecting southern and central Arabia with the north and east. Several South Arabian inscriptions have been found at the site.

The modern village of Hinna, 15 km. NE of Thaj, contains the ruins of one of the recent historic bedouin settlements established by King Abdul Aziz. The name of **ikhwan**, or "brothers" was collectively applied to these nomadic tribal groups settled by the founder of the modern kingdom. The stone structures of the **ikhwan** village at Hinna exhibit the reuse of the ashlar masonry of an earlier substantial Seleucid settlement at the site, probably contemporary with Thaj.

EARLY ISLAMIC PERIOD

In early Islamic times the eastern region achieved special renown. The foundations of Jawatha Mosque at Hofuf, the earliest mosque built in the region, are reputed to have been laid during the first years of Islam (c. 635 A.D.).

The city of Hofuf itself, longtime capital of the historic al-Hasa region, boasts several architectural landmarks of its recent distinguished past. The earliest foundations of Ibrahim Mosque, also known as Qasr al-Qubbah, date to the middle of the 16th century A.D., and the building has subsequently undergone several expansions. The palace was used as a barracks during Ottoman rule. A picturesque domed mosque adorns the interior. Qasr Khezam, another historic landmark in Hofuf, is a fort-palace built at the end of the 18th century A.D. It functioned as a military cantonment under the Ottomans.

اطلال المبانى المتهدمة من قرية بنى خالد على
جزيرة المسلمية شمال الجبيل . تاريخها :
القرن الثالث عشر الهجرى .

General view of Musallamiyah
Island, showing the foundations
of a village originally built in the
18th century by pearl fishermen
of the Bani Khalid tribal group.

صور لاربعة نسور حفرت على قطعة من
الحجر الصابونى ، عثر عليها بجزيرة تاروت
قرب ساحل القطيف ، يقدر عمرها بحوالى
٤٥٠٠ سنة .

Carved steatite fragment depicting
eagles from Taraut Island, dated
to the mid-3rd millennium B.C.

منظر تفصيلى لاحد مبانى قرية بنى خالد .

A view from the interior of one of
the village buildings on Musallamiyah Island.

جزيرة جنا (قرب جزيرة المسلمية) : اطلال لقرية اخرى من قرى بنى خالد . وعثر بهذه الجزيرة ايضا على مستوطنات تعود الى الالف الثالث والرابع قبل الميلاد .

◄

Jinnah Island: Two views of a large fort on the north side of the island, built in the early 19th century. On the same island exist some third millennium B.C. and earlier prehistoric settlements.

اطلال مبنى المسجد فى قرية بنى خالد بجزيرة جنـا .

Arches of a mosque built inside the 19th century fort on Jinnah Island.

قرية الحنا (٨٠ كم غرب الجبيل) : آثار قرية قرية العهد استخدمت فيها كتل حجرية تعود لآثار الفترة الهيلينية (٣٠٠ ـ ١٠٠ ق . م) الموجودة بالحناه .

Hinna, site of a substantial Seleucid (Greek) settlement rivalling in size that of well-known Thaj, 15 km. to the southwest. This photo illustrates the abandoned buildings of one of the resettlement sites for the Bedouin built by early Saudi government.

Closeup of one of the houses in the recent village at Hinna, showing the reuse of the Seleucid building stones.

الحنا: بئر مرصوفة بالكتل الحجرية الضخمة ، يعود بناؤها الى الفترة الهيلينية .

A Seleucid well at Hinna, still in use today. The well-cut sandstone blocks are fitted together without mortar.

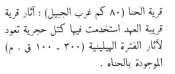

آثار ثاج من الجو :
وترى اطلال سور المدينة القديمة فى وسط الصورة ، كما تظهر علائم المبانى أسفل الصورة . وتبعد ثاج مسافة ١٥ كم جنوب الجناه .

Aerial view of Thaj, showing the outline of the outer defensive wall. Traces of house structures are also visible in the foreground.

كتلة من أحجار سور ثاج طولها حوالى المتر .

Detail of the construction of the city wall of Thaj.

أوانى فخارية من العصر الهيلينى فى ثاج .

Three Seleucid pottery vessels from Thaj.

كتلة حجرية من أحد منازل ثاج كتب
عليها نقش بالخط السبئى الحسائى .

Upside-down Hasaean Sabaean
inscription (c. 3rd-4th century B.C.)
on a prepared limestone rock,
reused in a building of the modern
village at Thaj.

فخار العبيد (بضم العين) الملون يختلط
معبقايا المحار المنتشر على سطح موقع
الدوسرية ، التاريخ : ٤٥٠٠ سنة ق . م .

Closeup of Ubaid surface debris
at Dosariyyah, including painted
potsherds, flint and shell.

موقع الد وسرية (جنوب الجبيل) : الجزء
المعشب على شكل تل صغير ، وسط الصورة .

General view of the Ubaid site of
Dosariyyah, 11 km. south of Jubail.
Site is visible in the middle ground
and measures 2 sq. km.

نماذج من فخار العبيد الملون ، من موقع
الدوسرية .
نماذج فخار العبيد من مواقع أخرى : على
اليمين – موقع أبو خميس (شمال الجبيل)
على اليسار : موقع العراح (شمال الهفوف) .

Diagnostic painted Ubaid pottery
(6th-5th millennia B.C.):
Upper figure from Dosariyyah site.
Lower figure left half from Abu
Khamis site, 60 km. north of Do-
sariyyah, along the coast. Right
half from Ain Qannas site - Hofuf
Oasis.

General exterior view of Jawan, a
Seleucid tomb complex 10 km. SW
of Ras Tanura.

Detail of the interior of Jawan
tomb, illustrating the cut-stone
construction.

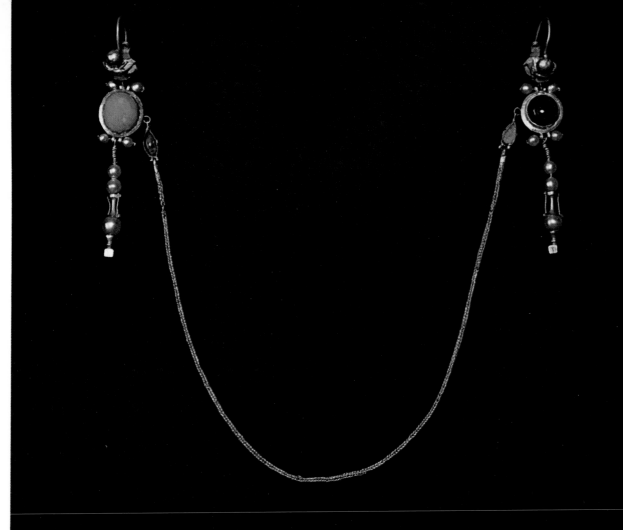

Two necklaces from Jawan tomb,
fashioned of gold and semi-pre-
cious stones.

قصر و قلعة عبد الوهاب بدارين (جزيرة تاروت) .

View of Qasr Darin, Tarut Island, from the sea. The fort is attributed to Abdulwahab Pasha and dated to 1302 A.H. (c. 1875 A.D.).

موقع سنابس (جزيرة تاروت) : وتظهر تلال المستوطنات الهيلينية و عليها آثار حريق .

General view of the burnt Seleucid settlement mounds at Sanabis on the northeastern corner of Tarut Island.

مدخل قصر عبد الوهاب و قد كتب عليه تاريخ بنائه سنة ١٣٠٢ هـ .

Detail of a door in Qasr Darin, showing the inscription giving the date.

آنية فخارية هيلينية من سنابس .

Glazed Greek pottery vessel from ar-Rafiah, Tarut.

قلعة تاروت : بناها البرتغاليون فى القرن السابع عشر الميلادى على أنقاض مستوطنات سابقة تعود أقدمها الى خمسة آلاف سنة ماضية.

Portuguese fort and tell at Tarut town, Tarut Island. Remains of earlier (3rd-1st mill. B.C.) structures are visible on the lower and middle slopes of the tell.

منظر من الجو لقصر عبد الوهاب بدارين .

Qasr Darin, Tarut, from the air.

تحف أثرية من تاروت يعود جميعها الى
٤٥٠٠ سنة سابقة :
صورة أسد منقوشة على قطعة من الحجر
الصابوني .
صورتان لوجه انسان ووجه أسد خلفه على
جزء من آنية حجرية .

Artifacts from Tarut:
Carved steatite fragment with representations of a lion and a
human head.
From left to right: two plain steatite vessels, a black-on-gray painted
pottery vessel, and two carved
steatite vessels.
Rim fragment of a carved steatite
vessel depicting a snake and the
head of a human figure.
(All are of 3rd millennium B.C.
date except for the plain steatite
vessels.)

تمثال حجرى يشبه التماثيل السومرية التى يعود تاريخها الى ٥٠٠٠ سنة سابقة . عثر عليه بجزيرة تاروت قرب القلعة .

Typical Sumerian (Mesopotamian) style statue of the early-mid third millennium B.C., found on Tarut Island.

مدافن منجم الملح (جنوب أبقيق) : شيدت
من الحجارة وأقيمت على هضبة صخرية ،
التاريخ : ٤٦٠٠ سنة سابقة .

Rock-covered tumuli containing
circular stone tombs crown a limestone terrace near Abqaiq. Original construction of the majority of
the tombs (which number in the
thousands) dates to the third millennium B.C.

أوانى فخارية كبيرة من مدافن منجم الملح
تعود الى نفس الزمن .

Two pottery vessels found in an
Abqaiq tomb which closely re-
semble third millennium B.C. types
from Mesopotamia.

بقايا مسجد جواثا (شمال شرقي الهفوف) : أقدم مسجد فى شرق الجزيرة ، أسس فى مستهل القرن الأول الهجرى .

Five small arches of mud-brick are all that remain of Jawatha Mosque in al-Hasa Oasis, the earliest mosque in east Arabia, founded c. 635 A.D. The visible ruins probably date to around the 9th century A.D., however.

مسجد الجبرى بالهفوف : يمتاز بمئذنته الجميلة ، وقد أنشئ سنة ٨٨٠ هـ .

Interior view of Gobri Mosque, Hofuf, dated to c. 1450 A.D., showing the *mihrab* (niche where the *imam*, or prayer-leader, stands) on the left, and the *minbar* (resembling a pulpit) on the right.

Mosque inside Qasr Ibrahim, Hofuf Oasis. The original construction of palace and mosque dates
to 1558 A.D., but they have been
expanded several times. The palace functioned partially as a military fort during Ottoman times.

منظر داخل قصر ابراهيم و يظهر أحد أبراج
القصر أعلا الصورة .

Qasr Khezam, a large palace in
Hofuf. Built c. 1800 A.D. and surrounded by a deep moat, it was
also used as a military fort during
the Ottoman Period.

مبنى البهو الكبير داخل قصر ابراهيم ، وقد
شيد القصر على مراحل كان آخرها سنة
١٠١١ هـ .

Large residential building on the
eastern side of Qasr Ibrahim.

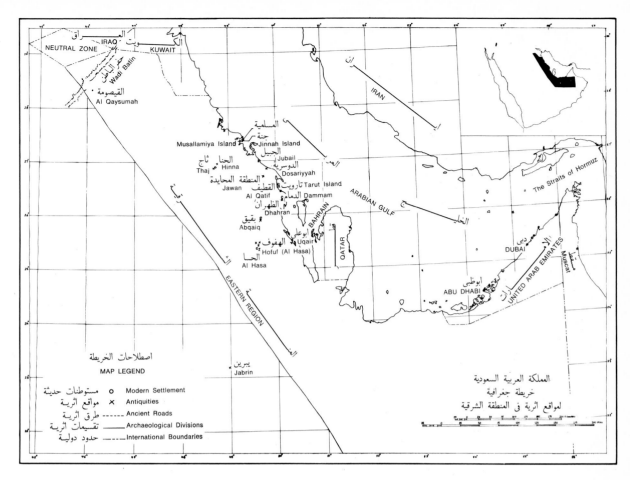

عريقة لاتزال رابضة تحت خرائب تلك السبخة تنتظر مكانها فى دنيا الدراسات والبحث العلمى . فيوجد بثاج مدينة متكاملة يحيط بها سور خارجى ضخم يبلغ طوله حوالى ٩٠٠ متر . ويرجع عصر بناء المدينة الى الفترة الاغريقية المعروفة بالعصر السلوقى ـ حاضرتها سلوقيا ـ فى جنوب بغداد بالعراق . ويبدأ تاريخ هذا العصر عقب فتوحات الاسكندر المقدونى سنة ٣٣٠ قبل الميلاد . وفى متحف ادارة الآثار توجد تسعة نقوش ضخمة عثر عليها بين خرائب ثاج ، وقد كتبت بالمسند القديم ويعود تاريخها الى أواسط الألف الأول قبل الميلاد . وعندما جاء الاسلام كانت ثاج مجرد قرية بعد أن انتقلت الحضارة التجارية منها الى هجر فى الاحساء . وعلى مقربة من ثاج ، فى قرية الحناه الحالية توجد أيضا بقايا لمدينة اغريقية أخرى تكاد توازى مدينة ثاج القديمة حجما .

أما الجرعاء ـ وهى حاضرة اغريقية مشهورة كتب عنها الكثير بواسطة المؤرخين الاغريق والرومان ، فانها من المعتقد أن تكون حول ميناء العقير شمال شرقى الهفوف حسبما دلت على ذلك بحوث البعثة الد انماركية فى عام ١٣٨٨هـ .

وباشراقة نور الاسلام الحنيف على ربوع الجزيرة تدخل المنطقة الشرقية بكاملها فى موكب الاسلام ويقام فى جواثا (تقع اليوم على بعد عشرين كيلومترا شمال شرقى مدينة الهفوف) مسجد يعتقد بأنه أول مسجد أسس فى شرق الجزيرة ، حيث يعود تاريخه الى بداية القرن الأول الهجرى . وتوجد فى الاحساء العديد من المعالم المعمارية التاريخية منها :ـ

قصر ابراهيم ـ أيضا يعرف بقصر القبة ـ وينسب الى الوالى ابراهيم بن عفيصان أمير الاحساء فى عهد الامام سعود الكبير . وتقدر مساحته بحوالى ١٦٥٠٠ متر مربع . وقد أقيم القصر على مراحل منذ عام ٩٧٤هـ وحتى عام ١٠٠٠هـ والبناء يجمع بين الطراز الحربى والدينى بحيث بنى بداخله مسجد تعلوه عدة قباب ومئذنة ذات طراز جميل .

قصر خزام ـ شيد فى عام ١٢٢٠هـ . فى عصر الامام سعود بن عبد العزيز الكبير . وتقدر مساحة القصر بحوالى ١٢٠٠٠ر متر مربع ، يغلب عليه الطابع الحربى حيث استخدم كثكنة عسكرية (ابان الحكم العثمانى فى الاحساء).

البديهى أن تنعكس آثار تلك الاسهامات فى أرض المنطقة ذاتها على شكل مستوطنات ومخلفات تؤكد نتيجة ذلك العطاء عند ما قامت حضارات زاهية على طول الساحل الشرقى وماسامته من الأرض وخصوصا نحو الشمال حيث تمخضت عنها حضارة سومر التى تعود الى الألف الخامس قبل الميلاد والتى كانت المقدمة الأولى للحضارة الانسانية بين النهرين . أما فى الشمال الشرقى لمنطقة الخليج ، فهناك مركز الحضارة العيلامية (الفارسية القديمة) التى تعود الى نفس الفترة والتى قامت فى (سوزا) وما جاورها من بلاد فارس ، حيث التقت شرقا بحضارة نهر السند الشهيرة بحضارة موهنجودارو والتى لازال العلماء يختلفون كثيرا فى تحديد نشأتها وامتدادها . وعلى الأرجح فان تاريخها يرجع الى ما قبل ٤٥٠٠ سنة تقريبا . وبالطبع فان جميع هذه المناطق الحضارية ظلت مع المنطقة فى اطار تبادل تجارى وثقافى عبر القرون حسبما أوضحت ذلك الأبحاث والدراسات الحديثة التى قامت فى أقطار ساحل الخليج وشماليه وشرقيه .

جزيرة تاروت :

جزيرة تقع على الخليج العربى مما يلى القطيف بالمملكه ، وتتصل بالقطيف بجسر طبيعى يتراوح عرضه بين ١٠ ،٢٠ مترا فى طول أربعة كيلومترات . أما مساحة الجزيرة فلا تزيد على أربعة كيلومترات مربعة ، وتقع مدينة تاروت التاريخية فى قلب الجزيرة ومن أهم مرافئها : سنابس فى الشرق ودارين فى الطرف الجنوبى .

وقد اكتشفت بالجزيرة آثار هامة يرجع بعضها الى فترة عصر فجر السلالات الأولى لبلاد مابين النهرين (أى قبل مدة تتراوح بين ٤٠٠٠ و ٥٠٠٠ عام) ، أما البعض الآخر فيعود الى فترات زمنية مختلفةمعاصرة للحضارة العيلامية الفارسية ، وحضارة الموهنجودارو على نهر السند ، وحضارة أم النار التى قامت بالمنطقة الجنوبية من الخليج العربى والتى تم اكتشاف بقاياها فى أبو ظبى بواسطة البعثة الد نمركية سنة ١٩٦٦.

أما بالنسبة للعصور الزمنية القديمة التى سبقت نشوء الحضارات فقد عثربالمنطقة على عديد من المستوطنات التى تعود الى فترة العصر الحجرى وماتلاه من الأزمنة التى تطورت خلالها حياة الاستقرار وصنع الفخار ، وتنتشر مواقع العصر الحجرى فى كل من واحة ييرين فى جنوب المنطقة الشرقية وعلى مشارف الربع الخالى ، وكذلك فى الجزء الشمالى من المنطقة وعلى امتداد وادى الباطن . ففى ييرين عثر على مواقع من العصر الحجرى الحديث الذى يعود الى فترة عشرة آلاف سنة سابقه .

كل تلك الدلائل المشار اليها تؤكد ماسلفناه عن قيام تبادل ثقافى مع البلدان المجاورة . وهو نفس مايستفاد من الأبحاث الأثرية التى اجريت فى واحة القطيف والاحساء والتى أسفرت عن وجود مواقع سكنية تعود الى ماقبل القرن السادس قبل الميلاد وتتصف بانتمائها الى عصر العبيد (بضم العين) الذى نشأ فى جنوب بلاد مابين النهرين (العراق حاليا) وكون القاعدة الأساسية التى بنيت عليها حضارة السومريين هناك .

فعلى مقربة من قرية المراح بالاحساء ـ مثلا ـ عثر على موقع من عصر العبيد يتكون من طبقات سكنية متعددة يعود قديمها الى فترة العصر الحجرى الحديث ، الأمر الذى يدعو الى الاعتقاد بأن ثقافة العبيد نفسها تطورت ثم انتشرت شمالا الى بلاد ما بين النهرين . ويؤكد هذا الاعتقاد اكتشاف مواقع من عصر العبيد تعود الى فترات زمنية لاحقة فى كل من منطقة الدوسريه جنوب أبو خميس بمنطقة رأس الزور ، ثم على الجزر المتاخمة للساحل مثل جزيرة المسلمية وجنا .

وبنهاية عصر العبيد قبل ٥٥٠٠ عام تقريبا ، وابتداء العصور الحضارية الكبرى فى بلاد مابين النهرين وشرقيها ظهرت أولى بوادر الاتصالات الثقافيه والتجارية بين مراكز الحضارة المحيطة بالخليج العربى ، وكما أوضحنا آنفا دور المنطقة الشرقية فى تلك العلاقات ، فقد استمر هذا الدور طوال مايقرب من ٣٠٠٠ عام ، وحتى الفترة الهيلينية (السلوقية ـ الاغريقية) والتى تفصح عنها عدة معالم بالمنطقة فى ثاج وجاوان والجرهاء وان كانت الأخيرة لايزال موقعها الحقيقى لم يحدد بعد تحديدا كاملا .

ثاج :

وتقع ثاج حوالى ٨٠ كم غربى مدينة الجبيل وهى اليوم عبارة عن قرية صغيرة على طرف السبخة المعروفة بسبخة ثاج . وقد أشارت البحوث التى قامت بها البعثة الدانماركية عام ١٣٨٨هـ الى أن حضارة انسانية

تكاد تكون آثار الاستيطان البشرى فى المنطقة الشرقية من المملكه أكثر وضوحا منها فى أى جزء آخر بالمملكة ،
وسبب ذلك يرجع الى عدة عوامل أهمها اشتهار المنطقة لتوسطها بين مراكز الحضارات القديمة واشرافها على جزء
كبير من ساحل الخليج العربى الذى سبق أن لعب دورا هاما فى مجال الاتصالات البشرية والتجارية بين شعوب تلك
الحضارات منذ أكثر من خمسة آلاف سنة . فقد انطلقت من شرق الجزيرة اشعاعات ثقافية امتزجت مع
ثقافات الاقطار المجاورة ، فتكونت منها دوائر حضارية كانت ذات شأن فى تاريخ الشرق القديم . وكان من

The central region
Nejd and Qasim

The expanses of the central plateau of Nejd, inclusive of Qasim to the north, and bordered by the Empty Quarter on the south, the Summan escarpment on the east, and the Hejaz mountains on the west, embrace the cultural core of Arabia. Ironically, it is precisely in this region that records of antiquities and early settlements are at the present most ambiguous, if not lacking altogether.

Riyadh (the present capital of the kingdom) and its adjoining oases (such as al-Kharj) were the center of the historic Yamama Region. Still earlier, these combined oases appear to have been inhabited by Thamudic peoples, as attested by several cave sites east of Riyadh which contain inscriptions dated to at least the 3rd century B.C. Burma Cave, located 30 km. to the north of the Riyadh-Dhahran highway, is a notable example of such.

DARIYYAH

At the present time Dariyyah is a small oasis-town located on the Wadi Hanifa, just 15 km. NW of the capital city of Riyadh. The modern town is situated mainly on the south bank of the wadi. Historically, however, the settlement embraced both sides of the wadi, the two sides being connected by a nearly 7 km.-long fortification wall. The area of old Dariyyah is now in almost complete ruin, with most of the buildings razed to the foundation. On the northern bank, however, in the former main settlement of al-Turaif, the remains of some impressive architecture still stand.

The earliest settlement at Dariyyah, that of Ghasiba on the south bank of the wadi, dates back to the 9th century A.H. (c. 15th century A.D.). The town's historic efflorescence did not occur, however, until the mid-12th century A.H. (c. mid-18th century A.D.), when Dariyyah became the focal point for the historic religious reform movement led by Imam Mohammad Ibn Abdul Wahab, a cause which received the political support of the then ruling Saudi dynasty under Emir Mohammad Ibn Saud.

The growth and expansion of the town was abruptly arrested around 1234 A.H. (c. 1819 A.D.) when it was invaded and destroyed by the Egyptians at the instigation of the Ottoman Empire. This date provides the **terminus ante quem** for the ruins at Dariyyah.

DWADMI

This is a complex of oases some 300 km. east of Riyadh noted for its many ancient sites. Among these are:
1. Jebel Baidhatain: This is an outcrop 13 km. east of Dwadmi adorned with Thamudic inscriptions and graffiti and containing the ruins of an ancient settlement of uncertain date at its base.
2. Jebels Khanugah and Barragah: These jebels, located 15 and 30 km. north of Dwadmi, respectively, are noted for their stone-built tombs and enigmatic ancient stone circles.
3. Wadi Masil: This wadi, located 50 km. SE of Dwadmi, is the site of some very important inscriptions. One of these records the campaign of the King of Saba against a local group of people in 516 A.D. The graffiti adorning many of the cliff faces along the wadi include representations of a multitude of known animals, as well as those of some mythical creatures.
4. Fau: Located c. 600 km. south of Riyadh in the Wadi al-Dawasir area, Fau is the site of a famous ancient city of central Arabia. The city once lay on an important trade route between Saudi Arabia and the regions to the north and east. Substantial remains of the commercial center of the site have recently been uncovered as a result of the research efforts of Dr. Abdulrahman al-Ansari of the University of Riyadh. The city is presumed to date to as early as the 4th (and possibly the 5th) century B.C.

Qasr Marid, a fort built c. 150
years ago, located 60 km. east of
Buraidah, Qasim.

قصر المصمك : ابرز المعالم التاريخية فى مدينة
الرياض بافتتاحه سنة ١٣١٩ وضع المغفور له
الملك عبد العزيز اللبنة الاولى نحو تأسيس
المملكة العربية السعودية .

Masmak, a historic fort and
palace complex in Riyadh, is the city's
most important architectural landmark, associated as it is with the
1902 conquest by King Abdulaziz.

جزء من مدخل قصر المصمك : وتبدو عن يمين
الفتحة الصغيرة كسرة احد الرماح التى
اصابت المدخل عند افتتاح القصر .

Masmak: detail of the doorway
through which King Abdulaziz
stormed when he captured the
city. Note spear point still em-
bedded in the wood directly to the
right of the open guard-portal.

قصر الامير محمد بن عبد الرحمن في عتيقة ،
احدى ضواحي الرياض ، أنشئ حوالي سنة
١٣٤٠هـ .

Palace of Mohammed bin Abdul-rahman in Utaigah, a suburb of Riyadh, one of the principal traditional palaces still standing in the city. Built of mudbrick, it illustrates the typical crenulated design on walls and towers.

منظر داخلي لقصر الامير محمد بن عبد
الرحمن .

Interior view of the above palace.

منظر شامل لاطلال حي الطريف بالدرعية
(٢٠ كم شمال غربي الرياض) حيث انطلقت
دعوة الامام المصلح الشيخ محمد بن عبد
الوهاب .

General view of the main street of at-Turaif, the principal district of 18th-19th century Dariyyah, which contained the residences of the al-Saud rulers and their retinue, as well as government buildings, forts, castles and stables.

موقع جبل برمة (٦٥ كم شرقي الرياض) :
نقوش ثمودية تعود الى القرن الرابع او الخامس
ق . م .

Graffiti on ironstone boulders which once formed part of rectangular-shaped tombs at Jebel Burma, 65 km. east of Riyadh.

جبل برمة : رسم الماعز
رسم لجمل

◀

Details of graffiti at Jebel Burma. Goat, camel and ostrich.

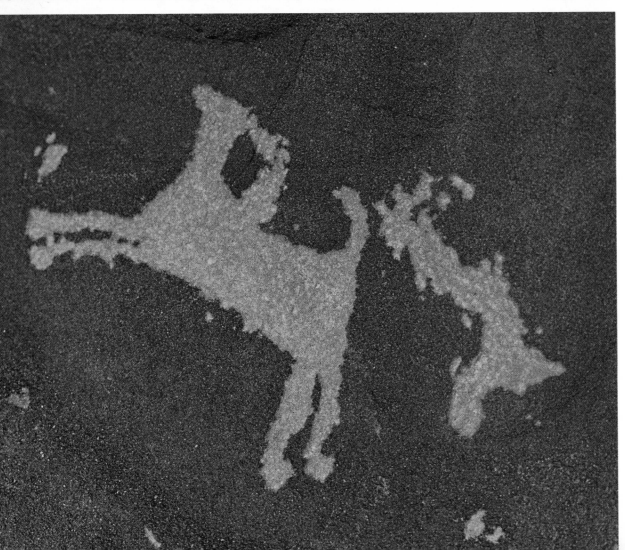

نقش ثمودي ــ نجدى

▶

Broken slab bearing Thamudic graffiti, also at Jebel Burma.

الدرعية : منظر شامل للواحة ويظهر احد ابراج المدينة القديمة فوق مرتفع حى الطرف . يرجع تاريخ تأسيس المدينة الى القرن التاسع الهجرى .

Dariyyah: view of Wadi Hanifa, showing the modern oasis settlement, with two watch-towers of old Dariyyah situated on the escarpment above the wadi.

قصر الفصاصمة بالدرعية : وتظهر أساسات البناء بالحجر يعلوها الطين .

Fasasma Palace (on the right) and adjoining buildings in old Dariyyah. The palace belonged to one of the notable families in the Turaif District.

قصر سعد بالدرعية : كان مقرا لاقامة الحاكم .

Qasr Saad, the main administrative/residential building in Turaif.

جبل براقة (الدوادمى) : مدفن دائرى عثر
بجانبه على نقوش ثمودية من القرن الثانى
ق . م .

Circular pre-Islamic tomb, built of
semi-prepared boulders, at Jebel
Barraga, c. 70 km. west of Dwadmi.

جبل براقة : بقايا مبانى حجرية على شكل
دوائر بالقرب من موقع المدافن .

Series of ancient stone circles of
unknown date at the base of Jebel
Barraga.

رسوم منحوته على جبل براقه .

Details of graffiti at Jebel Barraga.
Camel and *wasms* (tribal marks)
and wild goats.

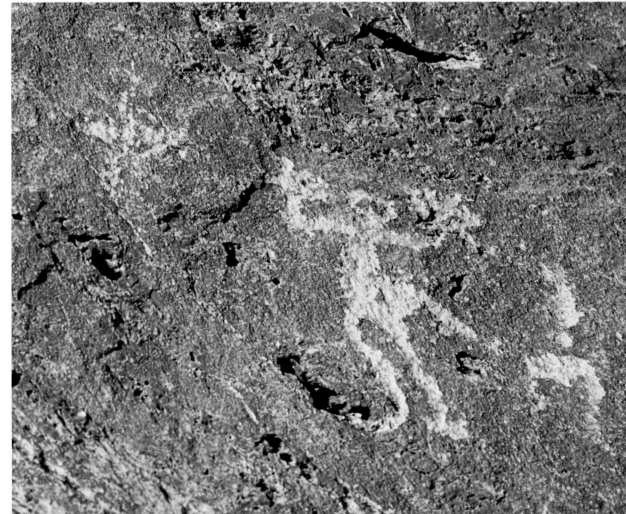

وادى ماسل الجمح (الدوادمى) صور لاشخاص
يبدو كأنهم فى مشهد راقص ويرجح ان تكون
هذه من المخربشات الثمودية ترتبط مع
النقوش الثمودية العديدة بالوادى .

Oddly-gesturing human graffiti at
Wadi Masil, 70 km. south of
Dwadmi.
Detail of human figure at Wadi
Masil.

جبل براقة : مناظر تفصيلية للمدافن الدائرية ،
والكتل الصخرية المصقولة التى استخدمت فى
تكوينها .

General view of tombs and graffiti
at Wadi Barraga.
Detail showing the prepared surface of a basaltic stone used in
a tomb at Jebel Barraga.

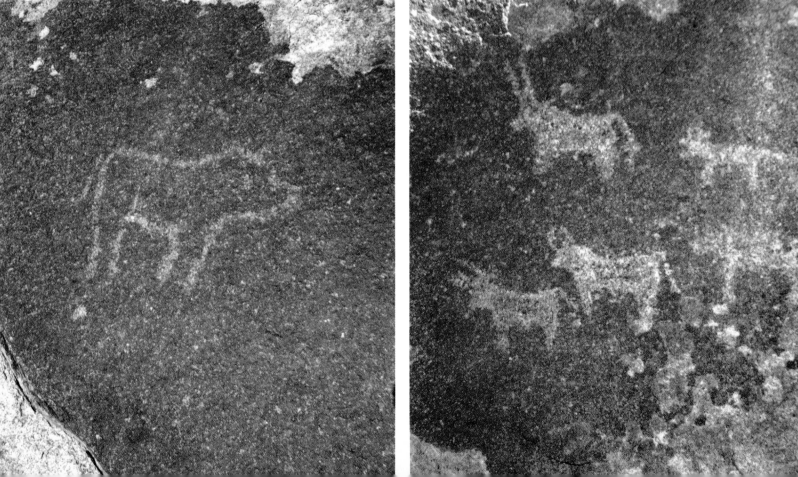

وادى ماسل : مناظر تفصيلية لرسوم حيوانية
ومشاهد عراك بين اشخاص وحيوانات غريبة .

Details of graffiti at Wadi Masil.
Ostriches and wild goats.
Man fighting a mythical animal or
lion.

جبل البيضتين (الدوادمى) منظر لصورة
خنزير وحشى ، وآخر يمثل صور حيوانات ذات
قرون طويلة شبيهة بالثيران البرية .

Details of graffiti at Jebel Baidhatain, 13 km. SW of Dwadmi.
Solitary figure of a wild boar.
Series of five animal figures of
uncertain identity.

نقش سبئى من وادى ماسل دونه ملك سبأ
وذوريدان وحضرموت ويمنات أثناء غزوته
للمنطقة فى القرن الخامس العيلادى .

A 5th century A.D. Sabaean inscription at Wadi Masil. It attests
the passage of a king of Saba,
Raydan, Hadhramaut and Yemnat,
who had built a castle to protect
the trade route and was now leading his army against the Saad
tribe in the area.

موقع الفاو (جنوب السليل) : منظر «التل الكبير» وتظهر خلفه مرتفعات جبل طويق . ويمثل التل واحدا من الاطلال العديدة التى تكونت منها هذه المدينة التجارية الهامة فى وسط الجزيرة العربية . ويعود تاريخها الى ما قبل القرن الثالث ق . م .

Al-Fau: general view of excavations in the commercial (suq) area of the site, with the Tuwaiq escarpment in the background. The site dates to the 4th-3rd century B.C.

نتائج تنقيبات جمعية الآثار (جامعة الرياض) فى التل الكبير . وقد تم اكتشاف مركز تجارى متكامل تحت انقاض التل .

Detail of excavations in the suq area at al-Fau.

آثار من الفاو (التل الكبير) : مقابض ابواب من البرونز على شكل راس اسد اوانى فخارية .

Artifacts from al-Fau:
Two bronze door knobs in the shape of lion heads.
Pottery vessels.
(al-Fau photos courtesy of Dr. Ansari of Riyadh University).

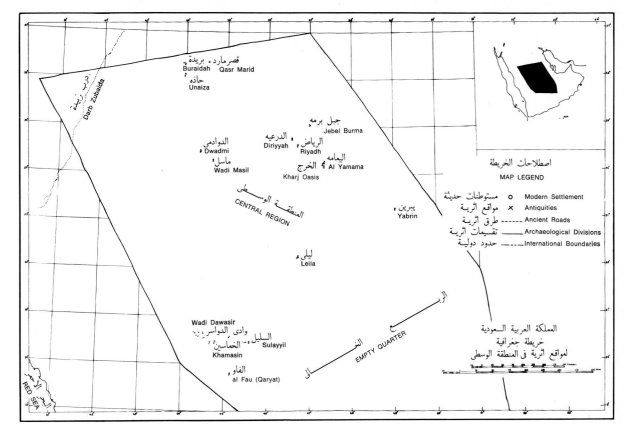

منظر عام لاطلال بعض مبانى حى الطريف بالدرعية (شمال غرب الرياض) .

Old Dariyyah: houses in the Turaif district.

Geographical Map of Archaeological Sites in the Central Region.

الثموديه . وعلى مقربة من الجبل توجد أبنية دائرية مثيلة لتلك التى عثر عليها حول جبل براقه .

وادى ماسل : يبعد عن الدوادمى مسافة ٥٠ كم الى الجنوب الشرقى وهو من أهم الاماكن الأثرية التى اشتهرت بوجود نقوش قديمة أهمها ثلاثة نقوش سبئية يذكر أحدها أبى كرب أسعد وابنه حسان ملكى سبأ وذوريدان وحضرموت ويمنات . وقد كتباه عندما خيما بوادى ماسل أثناء حملتهما على قبيلة (سعد) بنفس المنطقة . ونقش آخر يرجع تاريخه الى سنة ٥١٦ ميلادية كتب باسم معديكرب يعفر بمناسبة حملته ضد المنذر الثالث ملك الحيرة . أما النقش الثالث فقد جاء فيه اسم (تمم) أى قبيلة تميم .

الفاو : أهم قرية أثرية فى وسط الجزيرة العربيه تقع على الحافه الشماليه الغربية للربع الخالى وتبعد حوالى ٧٠٠ كم جنوب غربى مدينة الرياض ، بالقرب من ملتقى سلسلة جبال طويق مع وادى الدواسر . وقد قامت جمعية التاريخ والآثار بكلية الآداب فى جامعة الرياض برئاسة الدكتور عبد الرحمن الانصارى باجراء أبحاث أثرية هامة فى موقع القرية أسفرت عن اكتشاف العديد من البقايا العمرانية ، من جملتها مركز سوق كبير يدل على الدور التجارى الهام الذى لعبته المنطقة منذ أكثر من الفى عام سابقة .

ومن خلال ثلاثة مواسم تنقيبات أجريت حتى الآن بالفاو تم الحصول على كميات كبيرة من التحف والآثار النفيسة مما ينم عن مستوى حضارى بارز أحرزته المدينة ابان عمرانها .

قصر مارد بالأسياح : يقع على بعد ٧٠ كم شمال غرب بريده ، ويعود تاريخ بنائه الى منتصف القرن الثانى عشر الهجرى . وعلى مسافة ٦٠ كم شمالى قصر مارد يوجد سد مارد القديم الذى يحتمل أن يرجع تاريخه الى فترة أكثر قدما .

المنطقة الوسطى
(نجد ـ القصيم)

وتشمل العارض والوشم وسدير والقصيم ـ الخرج ـ ووادى الدواسر وغيرها ، وهى المنطقة الأولى بالنسبة للتقسيم الأثرى . وتكثر فيها التلال الشامخة ذات الكهوف والمقابر التى لم يجر التنقيب الأثرى فيها بعد ، عدى موقعا واحدا فى جنوبيها وهو «قرية الفاو» .

وقد لعبت المنطقة الوسطى دورا هاما فى التاريخ العربى قبل الاسلام وبعده عندما كانت تسمى باقليم (اليمامه) وكان يمتد نفوذها السياسى أحيانا الى حدود العراق شمالا واليمن جنوبا .

ومن معالمها الأثرية الهامة نذكر على سبيل المثال لا الحصر كلا من الفاو ، ماسل الجمح ، الدوادمى ، كهف برمة ، والدرعية ، قصر وسد مارد بالاسياح .

الرياض القديمة : يستشف من المعالم الأثرية القريبة من موقع الرياض الحالى ، خصوصا كهف برمة ، ومن النقوش الثمودية التى عثر عليها شرقى طريق خريص ، أن هذا الموقع كان فى الماضى القديم أيضا عامرا بالخضرة والمستوطنات الكثيرة ، وان الثموديين كانو يقطنون المنطقة وماحولها ، وأقدم نص عربى يتحدث عن الرياض كمدينة هو ما أورده ابن خلدون وهو :

ان قبيلة تعرف ببنى هزّان كانت أول من سكن اقليم اليمامة ، وان حجرا كانت مركزا له . وجاءت قبيلة عنزة بعد هوازن ، ثم ازدهرت حجر فى عهد بنى حنيفة واتخذ منها العرب سوقا كانت تقام فى المحرم من كل عام . وقد اتخذت الرياض القاعدة للدولة السعودية فى ١٢٤٠هـ عندما استعادها الامام تركى بن عبد الله .

الدرعيـــه : تبعد مسافة ٢٠ كم شمال غربى الرياض ، وتقع على جانبى وادى حنيفة ، وهى مدينة تاريخية عريقة يرجع تاريخها الى منتصف القرن التاسع الهجرى عندما انشأ غصيبه (أقدم أحياء الدرعية) مانع بن ربيعة المريدى أحد أقارب ابن درع صاحب حجر اليمامة . ومن يومئذ ظلت المدينة تنمو وتتوسع لأهمية موقعها الجغرافى وتوسطه فى الجزيرة . وفى منتصف القرن الثانى عشر الهجرى وصل الى الدرعية الامام محمد بن عبد الوهاب الذى وجد فى اسرة آل سعود ، وفى شخص الامام محمد بن سعود بالتخصيص ، خير مؤازر ومناصر فى سبيل دعوة الاصلاح واحياء السنة المحمدية . وهكذا أراد الله أن يجعل من «الدرعية» مركز هداية وايمان ومنطلقا لدولة شامخة الاركان .

وأشهر أجزاء الدرعية القديمة هوحى الطريف الذى كان مقر الأسرة الحاكمة . وتتولى ادارة الآثار حاليا مشروعا ضخما يرمى الى ترميم واعادة بناء بعض أجزاء الدرعية القديمة بما فيها الطريف بالاضافة الى السور والابراج المحيطة بهما .

كهف برمه : كماذكر أعلاه ، يقع هذا الكهف على مسافة ٦٦ كم شمال شرقى الرياض وتظهر على واجهة صخوره العديد من النقوش التى استنسخ اخصائيو ادارة الآثار منها حوالى ١٥ نقشا يعود أقد مها الى حوالى ٢٤٠٠ سنة سابقه .

الدوادمى : البجادية ـ وتقع على مسافة ثمانية وستون كيلو متر غربى الدوادمى ، وقد عثر بها على اطلال قديمة متهدمة وعدد من النقوش الثمودية وبعض المخلفات الفخاريه . وعثر بها أيضا على بعض خامات من الحديد التى تدل على أنه كان بالقرب من الموقع منجم للحديد .

جبل البيضتين : يقع ١٣ كم جنوب غرب الدوادمى . عثر على آثار مستوطنات قديمة قرب قاعدته ، كما تم الوقوف على نقوش حيوانية ومخربشات ثمودية رسمت على واجهة صخوره .

جبل براقه : يبعد حوالى ٧٠ كم شمال البجادية ، وجدت به بقايا أضرحة ومستوطنات قديمة تعود الى ماقبل الفى عام . كذلك تظهر حوله بقايا أبنية من الحجر على شكل دوائر كاملة لا يعرف أصلها حتى الآن .

جبل خنوقه : يقع على مسافة ٧٠ كم شمالى الدوادمى ، به كهف أثرى تظهر على واجهته بعض الرسوم والنقوش

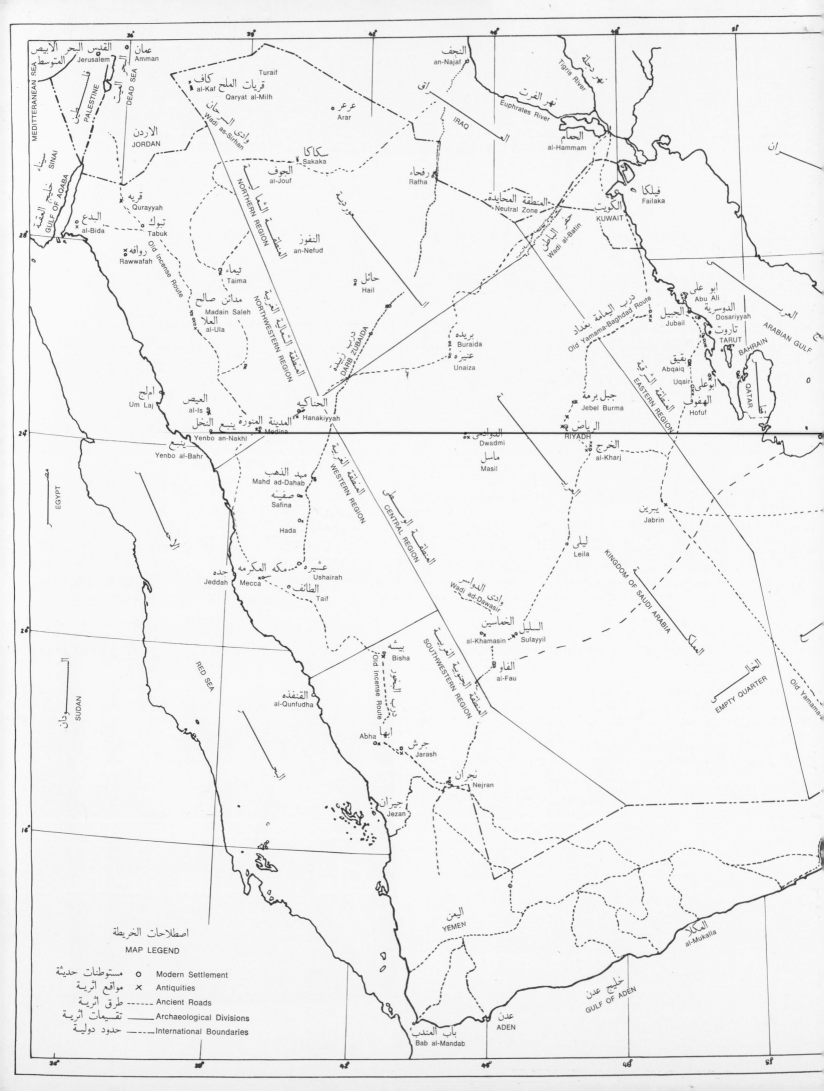